THE MAN IN THE ARENA

THE LIFE & TIMES OF A.C. SUTPHIN

George Condon

THE A.C. SUTPHIN FOUNDATION
Cleveland, Ohio

Dedicated to the memory of all of Cleveland's dreamers and unsung heroes whose collective efforts in the last two centuries have contributed mightily to their city's greatness

Photographic Credits: Editor, Ron Kuntz
Photographs of *Al Sutphin and the Sutphin family* courtesy of the Albert C. Sutphin Foundation
Photographs of *Gund Arena, Cleveland State Convocation Center, George Condon* and *Jeff Leitch*, Ron Kuntz
Photograph of the *Moondog Coronation Ball*, Hastings & Willinger
All other photographs, courtesy of CSU/Cleveland Press Collection

Book design, cover design and production: Patrick J. Powers
Manufactured in the United States of America

CONTENTS

On the ice at the Gund Arena

THE BRADEN. SUTPHIN INK COMPANY

In 1913, on the 5th floor of the Vulcan Building on St. Clair Avenue in Cleveland, Ohio, Jim Braden opened the doors of his fledging ink business. Within a few years he hired Al Sutphin, still in high school, as his first employee. By 1927, the name of the company had been changed to the Braden-Sutphin Ink Co. and in 1929, Jim Braden went into semi-retirement as Sutphin succeeded him as president. The company was now operating on East 22nd street, across from the Wolf Envelope Company.

When Al Sutphin built the Cleveland Arena in 1937 on Euclid Avenue, the new Braden-Sutphin Ink Co. was also erected – directly behind the Arena on Chester Avenue. It was operated there until 1957 when a need for additional space prompted another move to the present location at 3650 East 93rd Street.

During the last twenty years, that entire facility has been refurbished in a continued effort to provide customers with the best possible products and service at the least possible cost. Today, Braden-Sutphin has grown to include branch offices in Baltimore, Maryland; Cincinnati, Ohio; Detroit, Michigan; Indianapolis, Indiana; Pittsburgh, Pennsylvania; Buffalo, New York; Kenilworth, New Jersey; Richmond, Virginia; and a new facility built in 1992 at Carlisle, Ohio, specializing in web heatset inks. The company now employs over 200 people with annual sales in excess of $35 million.

Throughout its 80 plus years, Braden-Sutphin has been blessed with sound and dynamic leadership. From Jim Braden to Al Sutphin to Jim Sutphin, right up to Cal Sutphin and Ted Zelek today – the emphasis has always been on continuous improvement in every area: technology, manufacturing, quality, marketing, overall team management. So as the 21st Century approaches, Braden-Sutphin stands ready and committed to accept the new challenges that will face the graphic arts industry and is dedicated to maintaining their place as one of the pre-eminent American manufacturers of sheet-fed and web heatset printing inks.

THE A.C. SUTPHIN FOUNDATION

The A.C. Sutphin Foundation is incorporated in the State of Ohio under charter #823279. It's primary purpose has been to gather and compile into a published record, the history of Albert Claude Sutphin. The Foundation is operated exclusively for charitable, educational and literary purposes. No part of net earnings from these activities shall inure to the benefit of any private trustee, member or individual. Further, any net proceeds from the sale of this publication will be distributed in the manner provided under Ohio law for charitable corporations.

Overleaf: Albert Claude Sutphin

ACKNOWLEDGEMENTS

A book is always a group effort; the product mainly, in this instance, of many minds joining in recollection of one whom they love to remember. This book would have little substance without the especially important contributions of the loving daughters and sons of Al and Mary Hoynes Sutphin — Mary Elizabeth Sutphin, Jane Sutphin Leitch, Carolyn Sutphin Leitch, Alberta Sutphin Stoney, James Hoynes Sutphin, and Albert Carlton (Cal) Sutphin.

The crucial role of middle-man, directing the flow of information and coordinating the relationship between the author and his sources, was filled admirably by Jeffrey T. Leitch.

Grateful acknowledgment must be made of the indispensable help of friends like William Becker, Chief of the Cleveland Press Library at Cleveland State University; Patti Graziano, director of the Cleveland Plain Dealer Library; John Stark Bellamy II, Cuyahoga County Regional Library, Fairview Park branch; Patrick Powers, Ron Kuntz, Jane and Tom McManamon, Ruth Galvin, Jack Gibson, Lucille Garber Ford, Len Harsh, Jack Schmitt, Robert Leitch, James Leitch, James Krost, Ray Stoney, Helen Braden Scott, Greta Marlowe, Ann-Marie DeAngelo, Thomas Kelly, Victor Pergola, the Braden Sutphin Ink Company and Cook-Leitch, Inc.

George E. Condon

Webster's Dictionary defines the word "intermediary" as one who acts between persons or parties, in some instances even as an agent. Essentially, that is the function I attempt to perform in my daily life as a manufacturers representative. Being an "intermediary" for the purpose of having a book written and published, however, proved to be a completely different story. Because I knew literally nothing about the researching, writing, editing, publishing, and distributing of a book, this endeavor had more than its share of bewildering moments. On numerous occasions we wondered if we should even complete the task at hand. Fortunately, a most fitting answer to our questioning came near the end of our material gathering when we received a wonderful letter from Dr. Lucille Garber Ford, Provost of Ashland University. With her permission it is reprinted here.

There is, of course, no question that Al Sutphin lived life to its fullest. The matter of how he lived that life is even more extraordinary. The Champ's life had a powerful impact on eternity. Yes, eternity, because those lives he touched were lifted in a permanent, truly magnificent way.

I am one of those fortunate people so impacted, as are my children and my children's children.

As a little child, (I was the youngest guest at his wedding - 8 months old), I knew the world was beautiful when Al Sutphin came into the room. Good things would happen and, most importantly, each person in that room became special—loved and cared for in an unimaginable way.

My father O.M. Garber owned and built a large printing plant in Ashland, Ohio. He was a customer of Al Sutphin, and a life long friend. When "Uncle Al" (as I was instructed to call him) came each week to our home, it was a celebration. My father and "Uncle Al" talked business and dreamed dreams way into the night. (Neither one with money, they signed each other's notes at their respective banks!). Mother had a beef noodle dinner—the same menu week after week. He made her feel like it was a gourmet banquet. We anticipated greatly this dinner, filled with magic through Al Sutphin's presence. There was a special bedroom in our home where he stayed one night each week for many years.

These were the days Al Sutphin was building a highly successful ink business. His caring for customers was very, very real. He electrified customers by knowing their every need, responding to their problems (business and personal), by sacrificing himself. He cared about people. He shared with people.

When, at age 17, my sister, Mary Elizabeth (for whom Mary Eliza-beth Sutphin was named) died, the Champ was there. When I graduated from high school, the Champ was in attendance. When my father died at age 51, the Champ was waiting for me as I got off the train from college. When I was married, the Champ took me down the aisle. (He even wore a black tie!).

To customers, suppliers, employees—it didn't matter who, the Champ was always there. He had a heart that encompassed beauty, hope and grace.

These are the immeasurable things he gave to people - to many people. Of course, he gave generously with dollars, but he gave of himself. He made you special. You were loved. You could climb mountains—could overcome obstacles as he did again and again.

Al Sutphin respected all people. He was able to release the best in those around him. He listened and measured, he nourished and inspired. He gave each person he met a sense of worth.

In my home hang two pictures—one of Albert Sutphin and the second of Mary Sutphin—they were a tremendous team. As Al would reach out to others, "Aunt Mary" Sutphin led the response of support by an entire loving family.

Al Sutphin fulfilled beyond imagination his commitment "to make the lives of friends, associates and others just a little happier." The fact is, Albert Claude Sutphin not only achieved glory, he impelled glory in all those he touched.

Thank you, Lucille, for the inspiring words that motivated us to complete a project that had numerous starts and stops in the last four and a half years.

Jeffrey Leitch

Overleaf: Albert Claude Sutphin

PROLOGUE

The graven statues in any city's pigeon-roost pantheon of notables usually fit snugly in predictable niches. Most of the persons so honored and memorialized are selected from the ranks of politicians, perhaps even a few genuine statesmen, some military heroes, literary celebrities, classical music composers, pioneers, and a handful of inventors, city founders, pensive Roman philosophers and the occasional odd jurist of renown.

Whatever the reason for enshrinement, the eligibility rules for any city's hall of fame are fairly uniform. They usually demand of anybody under consideration a record of contribution to the public well out of the ordinary and significant enough in itself to demand a kind of marbleized curtain call.

Some underserving individuals, it is true, have slipped into the hallowed halls reserved for heroes by sliding under the outstretched rules like expert Limbo contestants. Conversely, there have been some deserving persons who failed to win the distinction because circumstances have dimmed or blotted out their achievements, or, more often, because the people's court simply failed to recognize the scope and value of their contributions to the society of their time. The system is fallible, and time itself is the enemy. Memory dims quickly and history is always in a rush, impatiently leaving a lot of unfinished business and overlooked heroes in its wake. Among these, in the Cleveland example, would be an uncommonly venturesome, generous, and colorful sportsman-businessman named Albert Claude Sutphin. His wholesome influence on the city's sport scene is felt to this day, long after his departure.

Sutphin, whose whimsical personal trademark was a bright red tie, was one of those human originals who cannot be fitted into any ready-made niche, especially one of those in the political halls. He was no statesman, no jurist, no diplomat, no influence peddler, no journalist, no academician, no professional do-gooder. He never made a speech except

Albert Claude Sutphin

Moses Cleaveland

under heavy duress. He hardly ever wrote a letter to the editor, except when he wanted to say something nice about somebody. His eyes skimmed past the heavy headlines bearing on national and international matters to seek out the sports pages and briefly, the business column. His major interests were linked by those two fields of endeavor: one fed the other.

Al Sutphin came to the attention of the wider Cleveland public in the beginning years of the historic decade of the 1930s, surely the most dismal period in the annals of the city and the nation. Until that time, he had been preoccupied in building up the fortunes of a small company, the Braden-Sutphin Ink Co., which had come under his direction at a time when other youths his age were attending college classes or struggling for a foothold in the working world.

Sutphin, who never even completed his high school education, was an outstanding salesman, a fact borne out by his achievements at the ink company, but his biggest challenge arose when he set out to sell his fellow-Clevelanders on the basic idea of deriving some fun out of being alive at a time when the world they knew had collapsed around them. He did this by putting together a pair of major attractions: A professional hockey team of championship caliber and a sports arena as grand as any structure of its kind in the country. It proved to be a winning combination professionally, financially and artistically, but more important on the larger scale was the mighty boost he gave the flagging spirits of a city that was wallowing in defeat for the first time in its history.

This is the story of a remarkable man who performed the impossible in an impossible time. But there was more to Al Sutphin than the hard-driving impresario of business and sports. Hidden from public view was the devoted family man, world traveler, visionary developer, good friend and generous host with a wonderful sense of humor. Among those who knew him best, his remarkable character rivaled his achievements and left an even greater impression. Memories are made of this in the life of Al Sutphin. They deserve to be relived.

There is no statue to mark his presence on the city scene or any memorial recalling his contributions to his city, his family, his friends and his associates, but then—who ever heard of a statue wearing a bright red tie?

Overleaf: Cleveland, Ohio, circa 1931

CHAPTER ONE

FROM PUGS TO PUCKS

At the beginning of the 1930's, probably the most fateful decade in American history, Cleveland was the fifth largest city in the United States and still counting. It stood at the trailing edge of boom times that had begun 70 years before and which had carried it from a lakefront hamlet into a metropolis that had doubled its population with every census taken.

That geometric rate of growth had an hallucinatory effect on the industrial and civic establishment. Growth and prosperity were accepted by the city's leaders as permanent blessings. A few deep thinkers in the academic community allowed themselves to speculate that some day the city might even edge out New York as the nation's most populous center.

Reality in the form of the stock market crash and the onset of the worst depression in American history dispelled the thick euphoria that had clouded the view of the experts and demanded an end to the fanciful speeches by the Chamber of Commerce types. It was trauma time, and with it the need for a painfully realistic reassessment of the new economic era for which nobody was prepared.

Clevelanders had already passed through a political crisis of sorts. They had decided to take leave of the city manager form of municipal government that they had embraced in 1924, the city's own noble experiment, and return in 1932 to the system of an elected mayor-city council.

The first elected mayor to take office with the resumption of old-line political rule was Ray T. Miller, a Democrat who had won public favor in his previous role as the fiery Cuyahoga County prosecutor. Among the least sensational of Mayor Miller's flood of appointments was his naming of Albert Claude Sutphin as chairman of the Cleveland Boxing and Wrestling Commission.

While his name was generally unknown on the larger public scene, Sutphin had made himself felt in sports circles as a journeyman-type baseball player who had advanced as far as Class A ball on the sandlots, as an enthu-

Ray T. Miller

siastic amateur hockey player who had held his own as a goal tender, but most of all as a supporter of all amateur sports.

Shortly after his appointment as the city's "czar" of the fight game, to borrow a quote from the sports pages, Sutphin further broke out of his background of near anonymity when he purchased the city's minor league professional hockey team, the Falcons of the International League. And even though the Falcons were anything but a high-flying team, Sutphin's acquisition automatically made him a principal figure in the sports scheme of things in Cleveland.

Hockey itself, professionally speaking, was a relatively new sport in Cleveland, and in the United States itself. The team, originally named the Indians, had been in existence only since 1929. They were organized that year by a popular sportsman named Harry (Hap) Holmes, who lost little time changing the name of his team to The Falcons to avoid the natural confusion of identities that had people wondering if the Cleveland Indians baseball team had taken to skates in the attempt to win games.

The year 1929 could not be judged as the best time for the beginning of any enterprise, except perhaps a pawn shop or a law practice specializing in bankruptcy. It was the worst possible time to try to popularize an unfamiliar professional sport like hockey. Indeed, there were so many adverse factors confronting Happy Holmes' venture that it was a wonder his team ever took to the ice, except for its own amusement.

Not only was the franchise under financed and under promoted, it had the additional handicap of playing its home games in an ice rink called the Elysium at E. 107th Street and Euclid Avenue, a facility originally intended for family fun skating and a few show-offs who knew how to twist and twirl while all those about them were doggedly trying to stay on their feet.

Harvey S. Humphrey, later the owner of Euclid Beach Amusement Park, had gained his initial fortune with a popcorn stand on the Euclid

Avenue site. So successful was he with that little business that he became known as Cleveland's "Popcorn King". But in 1907 he sacrificed the old stand by building the ice rink on the E. 107th Street corner. Interestingly enough, the land under the edifice was owned by Case Institute of Technology (now Case Western Reserve University), which leased it

Cleveland (1930)

to Humphrey. The Elysium, as it was named, cost Humphrey a whopping $150,000 and was said to be the largest, most elaborate skating rink in the United States at that time.

As the later setting for professional hockey, however, the Elysium was deplorably lacking. Its seating capacity was 1,900, and even that maximum had seldom been put to the test, although the building did provide a home for many years to a Cleveland team in the United States Amateur Hockey League.

Holmes did his best from 1929 on to win the patronage of Cleveland sports fans, but the reaction to a professional sport that was too new and too foreign, played in a small, icy barn, was nothing less than apathetic. The years of failure did little to make Happy Holmes a truly happy man, and his International League franchise was teetering on the edge in 1933, about to

Whitey Lewis

tumble into oblivion, when a Cleveland sports columnist, Franklin (Whitey) Lewis of the afternoon *Press*, came to the rescue.

Lewis, a shrewd judge of the sports scene and the people in it, had come to admire the city's boxing commissioner, Sutphin, and knew him to be not only an authentic sports supporter but also a fairly successful businessman who presumably had some capital at his disposal.

Lewis sought out Sutphin and advised him that the hockey team was about to go under and would fail unless a white knight—on skates, of course —came to the rescue.

The newspaper columnist made it clear he thought Sutphin was just the man for that heroic role. Whitey Lewis' timing was perfect. It was as though Al Sutphin had been preparing himself throughout his adult lifetime for just such an opportunity. His duties as the top executive of the Braden-Sutphin Ink Company over the previous 18 years had severely limited his own participation in sports as he devoted himself wholeheartedly to the job of building up the corporate enterprise. In this effort he had been so successful that for the first time in his life he was able to step back from the business routine and turn his money and energies to the other field he loved so much—sports.

The role of boxing commissioner did not satisfy Sutphin's ambitions. He was a true fight fan, but many aspects of the boxing and wrestling business revolted him. On the other hand, his recollections of his own hockey-playing days brought him nothing but pleasure.

What probably tipped the scales in favor of his buying the Falcons, though, was the fact that the franchise stood out as a failure. Sutphin had been a winner all his life. A losing hockey team represented a challenge that aroused all his instincts and could not be ignored. Biting down hard on the stem of his ever present pipe, Al Sutphin bought the Cleveland Falcons and took the big plunge that changed his life completely and altered sports in Cleveland decidedly for the better in the decades ahead.

The Elysium

Cleveland Falcons (1934)

Overleaf: Albert Claude Sutphin

CHAPTER TWO

BOYHOOD FOREVER

Within his own admiring family circle, Albert Claude Sutphin was famil-
iarly know as Champ. It was said that he disliked his given name, but
not enough to change it. He remained Albert C. Sutphin, or just plain
Al to the end. But the same permanency did not attach to his surname.
The United States Army, always a powerful agency for change, altered
Sutphen to Sutphin with a single stroke.

That misspelling came about on the discharge papers the army
handed the young Ohio soldier as he ended his two years in khaki with
the 135th Field Artillery at the end of World War I in 1918. Like any
smart serviceman, he chose not to make an issue of the mistake. When
the army hands you a discharge, you take it and run. The young veteran
not only shrugged off the misspelling, he accepted it as permanent, putting
him at orthographic odds with the rest of his family from that time on.

His parents, Carlton Ernest Sutphen and Elizabeth Pearl Thayer
Sutphen, clung to the traditional spelling, which originally was the Holland Dutch version, Van Zutphen, tracing itself to the family's ancestral
home, the town of Zutphen, Holland. It was from there that Sutphin's
ancestors traveled to North America in the 17th century, settling first in
New Amsterdam (New York), then on to Connecticut, New Jersey, and
eventually, Ohio.

The two small towns in southwestern Ohio in which Al Sutphin
spent his childhood are no longer on the state map, victims of urban
growth in nearby Middletown, which swallowed them over the years.
Franklin, in Butler County, was Sutphin's birthplace on April 11, 1894.
The family lived on Anderson Street, directly across from the paper mill
in which the father worked, before moving to a nearby hamlet named

Heno. Another move in 1900 took the family to Cleveland, where the father took a job at the Kingsley Paper Company and established a home on Lincoln Avenue, between Woodland and Quincy Avenues. At that time, young Al was enrolled in kindergarten at Lincoln School.

The Sutphins became lifelong Clevelanders with that move, but Al's ties with Franklin, Heno and the rest of the beautiful Miami Valley countryside were not easily broken. As a matter of fact, they tugged at him for the rest of his life. In the beginning, he was only a part-time Clevelander because he was allowed to live with his grandparents in southern Ohio during the long months of summer vacation, and those times provided him with some of his most precious memories. They were among the foremost thoughts in his mind in his last days as he started out to write an autobiography that only covered his youthful years.

"For eight years," he wrote, "I lived with my grandparents, both on my father's side and my mother's side, for most of my elementary school life. And although I do not remember Franklin very much in my early life, having moved to Middletown, six miles away, sometime before I was six, I had the opportunity in later years to know the town well. My life in Middletown encompassed two families, that of Grandma Thayer, who lived alternately on Vandeveer Avenue and the river residence on West 6th Street, and my Grandmother Sutphin [sic], who lived on Yankee Road."

The reference to his childhood evoked a heart swelling remembrance.

"What joys there are for a small boy living within the confines of a small, small town. Sorry indeed that my children, who were reared in Cleveland, Ohio, never had the advantages of a Middletown, a Franklin or a Heno, in their lives and were denied the joyous pleasure of growing up in a small town where on Saturday night the only thing to do was to go downtown where there was a popcorn machine on every street corner, and the usual drug store, where we had the best ice cream sodas imaginable. I say 'imaginable' because they always seemed so to me."

Such sights and delights of small town living intermingled with other recollections that came to Sutphin shortly before his death.

"Franklin, " he remembered, "was a whistle-stop on the Big Four Railroad, halfway between Dayton and Cincinnati. It was a town built on the Miami River and enormous hills overlooked the Miami Valley. I hardly knew Franklin at all in my early youth. I do remember Franklin over a period of approximately eight years, and did visit it through many years.

In Middletown, we lived on West Sixth St., the last house from Main Street, and also on Yankee Road. On West Sixth St., we were the first house facing the Miami River, which usually overflowed its banks and came up to submerging our home each spring. And in 1913, we became a disaster area." (This is a classic understatement, to be sure,

Al (second from left) loved his "small town" growing up

because the 1913 flood in the Miami Valley was one of the worst catastrophes in Ohio history.)

"Following the Miami River Valley," Sutphin's memoir continues, "was the C.H. & D. Railroad (Cincinnati, Hamilton and Dayton R.R.) and I spent a happy youth waiting for the nine o'clock train as it whistled for the Heno crossing. Heno was my entire outside world, and later, more than 60 years later, when I stood on great ships in Hong Kong, Liverpool and Acapulco, as I journeyed around the world, I still associated the sights of those great harbors with my days in Middletown, Franklin and Heno.

Exploring his early past, Sutphin's mind went back to the time "a great theater production came to our local Sorg's Theater in Middletown, and although later I was in New York to see *South Pacific, Show Boat, Call Me Madam, Oklahoma,* and other great shows, the production of a road show played in Sorg's Opera House remains in my mind as the greatest theatrical production of my life, a show featuring Charles Branden in the play, *When Knighthood was in Flower.* And although I saw thousands of great shows at the Paladium in London, Follies Bergeres in Paris, Moulin Rouge, also in Paris, and *Aida* in Rome, I still remember that Saturday night production of *When Knighthood was in Flower* as my most thrilling production. And the visit to Hartley's Ice Cream Parlor next door to the theater was my biggest theatrical thrill.

"Also, on each Fourth of July, came the inevitable fireworks display and all my aunts and uncles and other close relatives showered a small boy with gifts of small firecrackers (and) Roman candles...

Young Al & Family (1910)
standing, l. to r., Will Clark (uncle), Carey Clark (aunt), Ernie Sutphen, Al, Ethel
Sutphen (aunt, Ernie's sister), seated, l. to r., Edna Sutphen (aunt, Ernie's sister),
Louise Sutphen (grandmother), Elizabeth Pearl Thayer Sutphen (mother)

"Then, too, there were the joys of proud parading of all the civic bodies who annually appeared for the Fourth of July celebration, and what a pleasure to join such parades, proudly clutching a very fat grandfather's hand and being allowed to enjoy the great moments of the town's festivities.

"As this book is narrated and dedicated to my children, there will be many references [to] what Derbyshire and Berkshire Roads cheated them out of—the joys of living in a small town. Picnics in the Franklin Cemetery, Heno schoolhouse, and the 'Poor Farm' at Lebanon, also in the Miami Valley, just outside of Cincinnati.

"All these things happened 80 years ago, and I am fortunate that I have memories of those days. So far, this narrative is dictated of my life in

Franklin and Middletown, but later I will narrate the great athletes who ventured into my life and the great theatrical men of my time. And the wonderful life we led in the Cleveland Arena and with the Cleveland Rams and the Cleveland Browns ..."

Death, unfortunately, did not allow Al Sutphin to follow through on this summation of his life's experiences, but even as his voice trailed off in his final message, it had become clear that in this nostalgic return to the lovely, innocent days of his boyhood in the Miami Valley, Al Sutphin, the man of the world, had rediscovered a pleasure that may have been submerged by the passage of time, but which never was completely forgotten.

The old family farm in time became part of a golf course, and the town Heno, where his father played baseball 70 years before, became part of West Middletown.

Writing to his family from Yokahama, Japan, many years later, Sutphin said of the old homestead in Middletown: "I have never visited any place in the world, from Norway at the Arctic Circle clear to the tip of the boot that is Italy, and Southern Spain at Gibraltar, that meant more to me..."

Overleaf: Ever the ballplayer ... Al in his elementary school uniform

CHAPTER THREE

JIM BRADEN TO THE RESCUE

Young Al Sutphin led a double life during his growing up years. For nine months each year he attended Lincoln Elementary School and learned not only the basics in the classroom but also the way of life in the big city. But the summertime's long vacations were spent with his grandparents, the Sutphins and the Thayers, back in the small-town setting he so loved.

The result was a nice blending of experiences, as he himself was to attest during all the remaining years of his life. He found beneficial results at either end of the axis joining the Miami Valley to the Cuyahoga Valley.

Looking back on the vital 17-year period from the time of his arrival in Cleveland in 1900 to 1917, he concluded that it had been a "terrific" time; it had given him experiences and friends that stood him in good stead all his life and which he treasured to the end.

An extraordinary number of the youngsters in his own neighborhood and in the classrooms turned out to be lifelong friends, even as far back as his kindergarten days in Lincoln School during which he became acquainted with, among others, Frank Merrick (later a judge), Bill Finn (future fire chief), and such intimates as Albert Betz, Bill Reiser and the McWilliams Brothers.

He liked to dwell on the adult achievements of his old friends and neighbors, taking a personal pride in their accomplishments. He remembered, for example, that the McWilliams brothers had gone on to collegiate careers at Ohio University in Athens, where they helped to support themselves with a piano act in which they were joined by a college chum by the name of Frank Crumit, "whom they brought to Cleveland."

"He (Crumit) later married Julia Sanderson, who came to Cleveland as the star of the Ziegfeld Follies," recalled Sutphin.

Younger generations will be interested to learn that Frank Crumit was a talented tenor singer and composer who went on to national popularity on the radio networks in the 1930's, teaming with his wife, the equally popular Julia Sanderson.

(Not as well known is the fact that even though Crumit was an Ohio University alumnus, he wrote the words to the Ohio State University alma mater hymn, "Carmen Ohio.")

"During the days I lived on Lincoln Avenue," Sutphin wrote, "we became neighbors of Judge Frank Merrick, whom we called 'Punk' in those days, and I was eventually to become his political backer through many years during which we effected a fine friendship — a friendship that has lasted to this day, eighty years later."

Sorting through all the neighborhood legends that rushed to mind, Sutphin especially liked to tell the story of the Fleckenstein girl. Hers was a success story that gave all her Lincoln Avenue neighbors something to think about.

It seems that Mr. Fleckenstein's daughter, Rosie, ran away from home to take a chance on crashing into show business in New York City. There was the general opinion up and down the street that the young girl didn't have a chance. Terrible tales of what happened to innocent girls on wicked Broadway were passed along from house to house.

But then came surprising word that Rosie had landed a part as a show girl in a play called *Sis Hopkins.* Even more exciting was the announcement that the touring New York show had been booked into the Lyceum Theater in Cleveland.

Rosie Fleckenstein herself paid a triumphant visit to the old neighborhood, upon the show's arrival, to distribute complimentary tickets for the show to all her relatives and friends.

"I might mention," Sutphin wrote in his memoirs, "that although the tickets were free, the whole neighborhood was scandalized at the thought that Rosie Fleckenstein was a show girl and appeared with the chorus of the show.

"But, scandalous or not, we accepted her tickets and did go, anxiously scanning the program, only to find that Rosie Fleckenstein was playing the part of 'Sis Hopkins' herself under her theatrical name of Rosalind Fleck. And all of a sudden, our neighborhood was quite thrilled with her success." Rosie was a star!

Al Sutphin's adult reputation in Cleveland was that of being the hardest worker in town. It was said that he never went to bed before 2 a.m., and that he usually was on his feet, attending to affairs of the moment, by 6:30 a.m. That pattern of industry had its beginning in his boyhood years.

Central High School

"During the days of elementary school in Cleveland," he wrote, "I had many neighborhood jobs. Among them, I had a job under the custodian of Lincoln School whose name was Rory Grant. My job was to sweep the school down at the end of each school day, and consisted of sweeping the hallways and school rooms with a fine green chemical, and then sweeping the chemical from hallway-to-hallway, room-to-room.

"[I] also worked for Walters Florist at Easter time. Really never received a salary from the florist, who always paid me off in hyacinth plants for Easter, and which I proudly placed in a little wagon and delivered on Easter Day to the mothers in the neighborhood, and was proud as a peacock in so doing."

Upon graduation from Lincoln Elementary School, Sutphin enrolled in Central High School on E. 55th Street, a four-mile walk from his home. Not only was the academic load much heavier in high school, but young Al happily spent long hours participating in Central's athletic program, playing football and baseball on the varsity level. He also became a contributing member of the family by working at all kinds of odd jobs.

"During the summer vacations, I worked at the Cleveland Twist Drill Company, where I ran a lathe," he remembered. "My job was to polish drills, ten hours a day, six days a week, there being no child labor laws in my time."

Ed Bang

"And I will always remember the running of the lathe at Cleveland Twist Drill as the most boring of jobs; standing in one spot for sixty hours each week was most boring—so boring, in fact, that, perhaps once a month, our lathe room would receive a rousing cheer from the entranceway, and the reason for the great cheer was merely because the management had changed the size of our drills from big drills to small drills, or vice versa. Imagine cheering such an event!"

He liked to describe that job and that experience in later years to his sons as a kind of horror story to make them feel better about working in the shipping room at his Braden-Sutphin Ink Company.

Even in those early days, his natural talent as a salesman came to the fore. "As a kid," he once said, "I sold everything that wasn't nailed down."

In an interview with a *Cleveland News* columnist, Polly Parsons, he opened wide the book on his schoolboy enterprises.

"He took orders for cutting the lawns and hired other kids to do the work," she wrote. "He made and sold kites, owned two newspaper routes, ran his own lawn fetes. At Central High he simultaneously worked as sports correspondent for the News, made and sold belt buckles and worked in a meat market. He was goal tender on the hockey team at Central but otherwise couldn't afford the time for sports...he played both football and baseball as a semi-pro."

As a sports correspondent for the *Cleveland News*, incidentally, he came to the attention of Ed Bang, that newspaper's long-time sports editor, who never tired in later years of reminding the world that he had given Al Sutphin his first job.

It was a happy, busy boyhood, all things considered, but he was inclined to be rueful in later years when he reviewed his stab at secondary education.

"Although my grammar school was a great success for me, high school was very disastrous. In grammar school I functioned well with reading, writing and arithmetic, but when I got to high school and was exposed to physics, geometry and Latin, I became a total failure, and I lasted less than three years in high school."

It was a boyish prank that did him in.

The horrible memory of the tragic Collinwood School fire of 1908 in which 174 persons, mostly children, perished was still foremost in the memory of Clevelanders at that time. Out of that holocaust had emerged some strict regulations on fire safety in the schools, including the necessity of frequent fire drills.

Central High School was undergoing just such a drill one day when young Sutphin gave way to a clownish impulse. Perhaps in readiness for just such an event, he had purchased what was called a "Calico Cigar," an imitation of a cigar that blew "great smoke rings," he explained, "but there really was no fire at all."

With the fake, smoking cigar in mouth, he then "grabbed a derby hat that was hanging in the school room of the vice principal of the school, "donned the picturesque lid and sallied forth down the hall, completely unaware that he was under the glowering surveillance of the principal, Edwin L. Harris, and the assistant principal, E. L. Bathrick, who were standing on a balcony directly above. They saw no humor in the Sutphin spectacle.

"I was arbitrarily thrown out of school," he admitted, condensing into a few words what must have been an especially painful dressing down by the school authorities.

There was no way of understating the seriousness of the situation in Sutphin's young life. He knew the news of his expulsion from high school would have severe reverberations on the home front. Disconsolate over the turn of events, he boarded a street car and headed for that well-know intersection called Doan's Corner at E. 105th and Euclid, among whose busy stores and theaters was Cofall's Barber Shop, a neighborhood institution that served as a popular hangout for the boys from East High School, many of them Al's good friends.

What Sutphin had in mind that fateful day was getting some sympathy, understanding and advice from his chums on the corner, but on the streetcar he met a good friend of his father, James Braden, head of the Braden Ink Company. Al found a sympathetic listener in Braden, and he poured out the story of his high school escapade.

He confessed that the principal had banished him from classes and had ordered him not to return except in the company of his father. He told Braden he was not prepared for that ordeal and that since he really was not interested in continuing high school, perhaps the older man might be able to use him in some kind of job at the ink company.

Jim Braden

Braden, a warm hearted man, assured the troubled youth that a job at the princely salary of $5 a week awaited him in the newly-founded company. The executive furthermore kept young Sutphin's confidence and never passed on word of the boy's expulsion to Sutphen, Sr., a good friend of his. A year passed before Al unburdened himself to his father, also an understanding man. By that time the youth's foot was firmly planted on the first rung of a lifelong career in the ink business. Ernie Sutphen not only forgave Al the high school episode, he gave the youth a compelling reason to succeed.

Fate was kind to Al Sutphin when he poured out his tale of woe to Jim Braden on the streetcar that day in 1912. He couldn't have done better in choosing somebody to hear about his troubles. Jim Braden, it seems, was a kindred soul who had a deep, personal understanding of how it felt to be in scholastic trouble. He himself had experienced the same humiliating misfortune of being expelled from school — not once, but twice!

Jim Braden and his brother, Dave, had been booted out of the Ohio Military Academy, first, and then suffered the same fate at the Howe Military School, The reasons for the expulsions were never made clear. The Braden brothers, at any rate, rallied from that double scholastic setback by enrolling in the Culver Military Academy in Indiana at the time of its founding and were members of that famous institution's first graduating class. Jim Braden then went on to Butler University and graduated with honors.

Of all the counselors that Al Sutphin might have turned to when he was banished from the halls of Central High School, Jim Braden was the most fortunate choice.

*... near Middletown, young Al recovers
from an errant tee shot*

Jim Braden's dapper, young, salesman

Overleaf: Mary Althea Hoynes

CHAPTER FOUR

THE SOLDIER SURRENDERS TO MARY

The word to describe Al Sutphin in the prime of his life when he had assumed full control of the Braden-Sutphin Ink Company was "driven," but even that word hangs limply on the page in light of the sequence of events that led eventually to his liberation from the limited scope of an ink salesman-executive to the larger, more prominent role that he was to fill in Cleveland civic life.

The several years immediately following the untimely end of his high school career constituted a foundation time during which he learned the ink business, gave free play to his love of baseball and hockey, and cultivated a band of friends who gave him a lifetime of companionship. It also was a time, more important, in which he was to weld his romance with the love of his life, Mary Althea Hoynes.

The Hoynes family, especially in the person of Dan Hoynes, had already been an influence in Al Sutphin's young life from schoolboy days on. He and Dan played together on the sandlots, exchanged youthful confidences, supported each others ambitions, and were the closest of friends by the time they were old enough to go to high school despite the fact that they held to different religious tenets. Dan Hoynes was a Catholic. The Sutphin family was Protestant. Those affiliations led them into different circles of activity but never separated them completely or diminished the strength of their friendship.

Sutphin, in his unfinished autobiography, recalled that upon his family's move to Cleveland at the turn of the century, "my life centered mostly in the confines of Grace Methodist Church where, at fourteen, I took over many church duties. In fact, I was a 14-year-old secretary and treasurer of the church. We were surrounded by three enormous Catholic churches, although most of the neighborhood churches of the Protestant faith were small indeed.

"…Our lives after moving to Cleveland were confined by the Woodland and Buckeye Roads and Quincy Street in the neighborhood of Southern Avenue, Lincoln Street—and what great communities we had. This was during the years between 1900 and 1917.

Grace Methodist Baseball Squad (1912)

"Incidentally, during these eight years I organized a baseball team representing little Grace Church. We played in the East Side Church League and we won the city championship for seven straight years…we played city-wide churches and I bought excellent baseball suits from a very young, fast-talking salesman who was the representative of Spaulding's Athletic Store. His name was Dick Kroesen, and I was destined to buy from him all of our hockey equipment in the Cleveland Arena."

Sutphin's Grace Church team turned out to be a powerful ecumenical force in his young life as it brought him into contact with youngsters of other religions, especially in his heavily Catholic neighborhood.

"…[There] were two very large Catholic schools and churches, one known as St. Edward's and the other as Holy Trinity — St. Edward's being an Irish church and Holy Trinity a German church. And I grew into manhood before I knew the identity of St. Edward's and Holy Trinity. Through my youth I knew them as "Father Brennan's" and "Father Baker's."

"Although we played most of our baseball games against the two schools, we beat St. Edward's almost constantly....There was a third Catholic church and school in our neighborhood, St. Agnes, which was located on Euclid Avenue, whom we played football with nearly every Saturday morning, and I remember their quarterback, Judge Kennedy's son, as being their star performer. Saw young Kennedy often, and he claimed that they used to beat us most of the time, but they didn't—because we had one short, stumpy boy who had great

Michael Hoynes

ability, and when the boy, 'Pickles' Krause, was able to play, we always won. Later, Pickles showed up in my life again by joining my army battery in Pierrefitte Sur Aire in France... And Pickles came back to Cleveland to be a printer and one of my best ink customers.

The Sutphin-Hoynes connection grew stronger with the passage of time. Because the Braden Ink Company was having difficulties in obtaining necessary chemical supplies and had frequent work stoppages, Al went to work at Central Electrotype on Chester Avenue prior to the outbreak of World War I. It was no coincidence that Central was owned by Michael J. Hoynes, father of Sutphin's friends.

Hoynes was a well-to-do industrialist of Irish descent whose business had flourished in the heady days of Cleveland's boom times. His wife, Florence, who seemed to have been forever known as "Grandma Hoynes," was a descendant of the distinguished Brownell family. Her father was a respected doctor who had graduated in St. Vincent Charity Hospital's first class and served in the Civil War.

Originally from Akron, Michael Hoynes had moved his family to Cleveland in 1896, shortly after the birth of their daughter, Mary Althea, to a sprawling home on East 69th Street, a stone's throw from Millionaire's Row.

It was there that Mary Althea grew up, in a warm and caring setting, always crowded with friends, neighbors and guests. Each day the table was formally set for twelve, with white linens, crystal and silver. Hoynes earned a reputation as not only a shrewd investor who "owned stock in everything," but as a "kind, overly generous man." Florence

Mary Althea Hoynes

was equally well known as a patient, inexhaustible mother of five and a gracious hostess who made sure that dinner at the Hoynes' was an event and welcomed all forms of entertaining as reason for memorable celebration, from kids on the front porch for lemonade to elegant parties for a hundred. The next eighty years would show that Mary Althea Hoynes learned these lessons well.

At the time of Sutphin's employment, Mary Althea Hoynes, the teenage daughter of the owner, worked in the company office as a typist and receptionist. That summertime meeting of the two had lifetime consequences. Albert C. Sutphin admittedly was smitten by her beauty and fresh personality.

It was about that time that World War I altered the lives of all Americans. Sutphin, who earlier had some reserve army training in Cleveland's Troop A Cavalry unit, enlisted and, with many of his buddies, found himself in Battery D, 135th Field Artillery. Among those army friends was Dan Hoynes, and as might be expected, the book of family lore and legend was considerably expanded by the stories that came out of the two years that Al Sutphin and Dan Hoynes spent together in the army.

Young Dan Hoynes had to do considerable talking before he was accepted in a combat outfit by the army. He had suffered a bad knee injury and the medical opinion was that he was not eligible for combat, but Dan wove a fanciful tale of his culinary abilities that the army found irresistible. Good cooks are always in demand in the military. Dan, who actually couldn't fry an egg, was accepted. In later years, Sutphin's standing as a raconteur was considerably strengthened by the rollicking stories he liked to tell of Dan Hoynes' adventures in the outfit's mess, including lurid descriptions of the meals that were concocted by that amateur chef.

Even during his army years, Sutphin's interest in sports stayed at a high level. While his outfit was in training at Camp Sheridan in Alabama in 1917, Sutphin brought together and managed Battery D's baseball team. Under his managerial direction, his charges went on to the regimental championship.

Not much time was wasted on military training before the 135th Artillery was shipped to France and billeted in the vicinity of a small

Private Sutphin, still in the middle of things (2nd standing row, 6th from the right)

village just north of Paris, Pierrefitte Sur Aire. It was a center of some strategic importance at that juncture. From there, the outfit moved on to bivouac in an even smaller town, Neuville, close to the front line.

Many years later, Sutphin took his family to Neuville, and lined them all on the village bridge so they could drink in the scene, in his own words, of "the lowest point in my life."

He explained that on the day that his comrades of the 135th began to move on to the battlefield, he was left behind because he was ill. Sutphin said that the memory of that World War I day in which he felt "absolutely alone in the world" was still with him. But it was a memory, he told them, from which he drew courage during his darkest days in business in later life.

"No matter how bad things got," he said, "or how much money we owed, or how bad the hockey team was going — nothing ever could be as bad as that day in 1918 in Neuville!"

Sutphin's two years in uniform were a treasured experience and the friendships with the men of Battery D seemed to gain strength through the years of frequent reunions. Perhaps the most striking result of his World War I experience, though, was lifelong love affair with France, and Paris in particular.

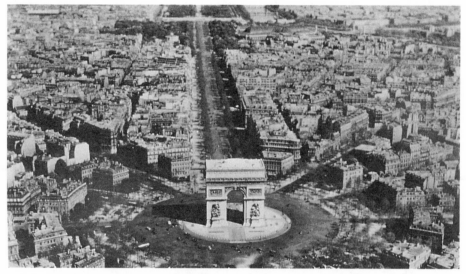

Paris (1917)

Beginning with a return trip to France in 1920 for the Olympic Games, Sutphin visited that country at least 15 times, perhaps more. His family simply lost count along the way. And while Al's tours encompassed all of France, the focus of his Francophilia was always Paris, which he considered the greatest city in the world.

He had a special place in his heart also for the villages of Pierrefitte and Neuville whose people had befriended him and his fellow soldiers.

His French friends became a branch of his personal family and he kept close track of them. Through the frequent exchange of letters and pictures, he also came to know their children and their grandchildren.

When the men of Battery D were mustered out of service upon their return to the U. S. in 1918, Sutphin returned and resumed his employment with Central Electrotype. No doubt he was drawn there by the presence of Mary Hoynes, but she was also the reason he quit his job. Jim Sutphin remembered his father's account:

"Dad went to Mike Hoynes one day and said, 'I'm going back to work for Jim Braden.'

"Mr. Hoynes said, 'Why? Don't you like it here? You seem to get along well with Paul and Dan.'

"Dad said, 'I get along fine. But I want to marry your daughter, and I don't want to be your son-in-law and your employee!'

"So," recounted Jim Sutphin, "it was back to the ink business for Dad. As a matter of fact, I have told people for years that if my mother hadn't married my father, I would have been an electrotyper!"

The Sutphin-Hoynes wedding party (1922)

After Al had removed himself from the Central Electrotype payroll, he felt free to pursue his courtship of Mary Hoynes and he lost no time pressing his suit to a successful end. Family legend has it that Al spent most of his courtship trying to get on the good side of Mary's mother, Florence. One particular Sunday, Al volunteered to take Mrs. Hoynes to Akron to visit relatives. Sutphin's car was old and the tires completely worn. The trip turned into a day long odyssey when Al had three flat tires, spent all his money repairing them, and finally had to ask Mrs. Hoynes to buy him two new tires.

Undaunted by this misadventure, Sutphin continued his efforts to impress Mike Hoynes' daughter.

Al had but one suit and very limited resources. He did have an unlimited supply of determination and diligence. It wasn't long before his hard work won the day.

The wedding of Mary Hoynes and Al Sutphin took place in St.

Philomena Catholic Church in East Cleveland on August 14, 1922 with Monsignor Joseph Smith officiating.

Al and Mary left immediately after the ceremony for New York City where they were to board the Cunard Line's great ship, the *Leviathan*, and set sail to Europe for their honeymoon. Dan Hoynes led a group of friends and relatives to Manhattan to see the newlyweds off with a proper celebration. It wasn't until the ocean liner was at sea that Al and Mary discovered that their well-wishers had filled the drawers of their wardrobe trunk with confetti!

Upon arrival in Paris, the groom bought his bride a ponyskin coat which never wore out and in the years that followed was passed along from one member of the family to another. The story is still told with relish that their daughter Alberta wore the coat on one of her first dates with Raymond Stoney, and that it so impressed him that he married her.

It was, by all accounts, a highly successful and happy honeymoon. Proof of that was that when the new Mr. and Mrs. Albert C. Sutphin arrived at their home shores in New York, they had only 25 cents between them, and Al had to wire his father for money to get back to Cleveland.

Their first child, Mary Elizabeth, was born the following year, on November 20, 1923. That timely arrival allowed the baby to be featured on the couple's 1923 Christmas card, their first one. It had been preceded by a card announcing the birth which said: "Jimmy's name is Mary Elizabeth!"

When Albert and Mary took their first-born home from St. Ann's Hospital on Woodland Avenue, it was a newly-built house at 2557 Derbyshire Road in Cleveland Heights, about two blocks east of the historic Alcazar Hotel.

Those were the foundation years for Al and Mary, with their new baby and their new home, and it isn't surprising that they went about the job of shoring up their financial basis at approximately the same time. In 1924, Al courageously borrowed the enormous sum of $44,000 from his Uncle Will Clark and his father which he used to buy 10 percent of the stock of the Braden Ink Company.

This fresh investment, added to the $6,000 worth of stock purchased in 1923, enlarged Sutphin's role in the company's affairs but he had afterthoughts many years later.

"The fifty thousand dollars I had invested was supposed to be 10 percent of all stock issued — but being young and not knowing too much of the business world, I thought it a good deal," Al wrote in 1966, 42 years later.

The Honeymooners arrive in Germany

"Years later, I learned that $50,000 for 10 percent of the stock was certainly a joke," he concluded.

Joke or not, it was another important step toward the top for the 30-year old sales genius.

Al & Dan Hoynes, lifelong friends

Mary Hoynes, August 14, 1922

The Hoynes Family, circa 1900
(Back row, standing, l. to r., Mary, Florence, Daniel, Paul
front row, seated, l. to r., Micheal, Dennis, Florence)

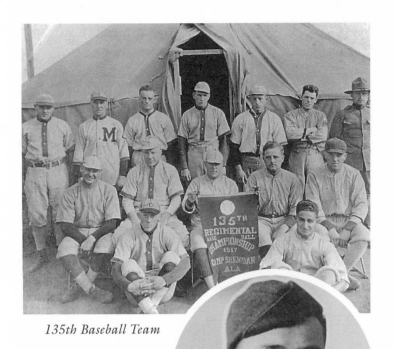

135th Baseball Team

Al & Friend
Camp Sheridan, AL

Pierrefitte su Aire (1917)

Overleaf: The Growing Sutphin Family l. to r., Carolyn, "baby" Jim, Jane, Mary Elizabeth & Alberta

CHAPTER FIVE

BIRTH OF A FAMILY, DEATH OF A FRIEND

That decade from 1920 to 1930, familiarly identified as the "Roaring Twenties," was a period of postwar unrest and social change; the time in which the idealistic concept of Prohibition was tested and found wanting and the time in which sports stars and gangsters shared the front pages.

The young people of that singular period usually are depicted as social rebels whose women wore short skirts and bobbed hair and were bold enough to puff cigarettes in public, and whose men wore bell-bottom trousers, grew long sideburns à la Valentino and slicked back their hair with greasy tonics. Both sexes, of course, spent their dissolute hours dancing the Charleston and drinking hootch in speakeasies. Theirs was a merry, amoral life.

It wasn't that way with the newlyweds, Al and Mary Sutphin. They chose an entirely proper, traditional way of life which allowed little time for high jinks. One compelling reason for their preoccupation with home life was their steadily growing family. Mary Elizabeth, born in 1923, was soon followed by Florence Jane (1925), Carolyn Alberta (1927), Alberta Ernestine (1928), James Hoynes (1932) and Albert Carlton (1939).

The place on Derbyshire became a full house as time went on except for one important element: The father of the brood was usually missing when it came time for a head count.

If many of the men his age were having a boisterous good time during the 1920's, Al Sutphin was putting those years to the best possible use in the pursuit of a state of financial well-being that would assure him, and his growing family, of a worry-free future.

His nickname of "Champ" was no empty compliment. He was so intent on success that he allowed his job to claim the major share of his attention. At one time in this critical period of growth, he took stock of his life and discovered that he had been spending as many as 250 days a year on the road, and had maintained this unrelenting pace since he and his wife had returned from their honeymoon.

The 1920's, the era of prohibition

This was an impatient man with a mission. Against a background of such single-minded effort, his participation in family counsels had to be a sometime thing. His family could never be sure that he would be home for dinner, or even if he would be home at all on a given night or a given week.

What they could be sure of was Mary Hoynes Sutphin. She was always there, the complete mother and complete wife. She gave the children the guidance they needed and the moral precepts that ruled her own life. And she gave her husband the anchorage he needed, in a home port where love abounded.

Al Sutphin's master plan for success worked out, just as he knew it would. His formula of hard work and smart management, buoyed by his own extraordinary talent for salesmanship, was unbeatable. In 1927, the corporation changed its name to the Braden-Sutphin Ink Company in recognition of his stock ownership and vital sales contribution and the enterprise continued to flourish.

Jim Braden was aware of his junior partner's ambition, recognized him as the catalyst of the company's ascendancy and appreciated the fact that having Sutphin on hand as his successor fit in nicely with his own long-range plans. He was older than Sutphin by 15 years, and his per-

Mary, Jane & Carolyn (1928)

sonal blueprint called for early retirement. An avid outdoorsman and dedicated fisherman, Braden became less and less the ruling force in the company through the years as he spent more and more time at Braden Island, the family retreat in Canada, north of Georgian Bay.

The future plans of these two men meshed like a specially designed zipper. Sutphin wanted to buy the ink company and Braden wanted to sell it. They put their heads together and worked out a set of terms which allowed both of them to realize their ambitions.

"In 1929, when I bought Jim Braden out," recalled Sutphin years later, "I once more borrowed fifty thousand dollars—from Ora Garber, Joe Gideon, my father, and my Uncle Will Clark—and made a down payment to Jim Braden.

"Agreed in a contract to pay him thirteen thousand dollars a year for a matter of twenty years, and raised my salary so that I could make these payments. In fact, I never missed one. By this time I had four hundred thousand dollars invested in the Braden-Sutphin Ink Company. In fact, I was the only investor." Braden, who reached the age of 50 that year, was guaranteed a retirement income. A handshake settled the deal.

Oddly enough, the future careers of Sutphin and Braden found a common relationship in city politics. Mayor Ray T. Miller chose Sutphin to be boxing and wrestling commissioner while his successor, Mayor Harry

Braden-Sutphin (1922)

l. to r., Frank Baumgardener, Jim Braden, Al &Al Betz

L. Davis, called on Jim Braden to be the city's purchasing agent. As Sutphin left City Hall, Braden was on his way in.

It was an essential post that Braden was called on to fill, one made even more difficult than usual by the city's straitened finances in the steadily deepening depression. The mayor, the finance director, the city council and the public itself looked to City Purchasing Agent James Braden to keep expenditures under control.

Jim Braden had been a quiet, unassuming businessman and was not at all accustomed to the public spotlight and the searching attention of the daily newspapers. But, being a man of considerable aplomb, he took his newfound prominence in the same even stride which had marked his progress in earlier endeavors. His personal rooting section, led by Al Sutphin, was overjoyed to find Clevelanders of all political stripes discovering the fine qualities of the man they had known and admired for years. And nobody was more pleased by Braden's public success than his wife, the former Helen Fishter, and their two daughters, Helen and Eleanor.

Mrs. Braden, interestingly enough, had known public prominence and newspaper fame long before she became his wife. Dayton, Ohio was her home town at the time that a pair of townsmen, Orville and Wilbur Wright, startled the world with their successful flight in a heavier-than-air craft (an aereoplane, as it was called) at Kitty Hawk, N.C.

When the Wright brothers returned to Dayton after that epochal achievement, the city celebrated with a civic salute that was capped by an elaborate street parade. One of the central displays in the parade was a float carrying Helen Bertha Fishter, the queen of the celebration. She

The historic flight of the Wright Brothers

was draped in the American flag and held a small replica of the Wright Brothers' plane high above her head while thousands of Daytonians cheered and saluted.

Jim Braden met Helen Fishter a year after that parade, on July 30, 1909. They were married the very next day. The swift courtship and wedding probably set a new local record for such events, but their marriage, as it turned out, was a long and happy one.

As the city's purchasing agent, Braden went beyond all expectations in his control of municipal expenditures. Householders, for example, were told to lug their rubbish to the curb lawn; no more backyard service. Public beaches, playgrounds and pools were curtailed in their hours. So was the dog pound. The operation of bridges over the Cuyahoga River was cut back to save the wages of bridge tenders. Professional politicians, always fearful of voter reaction to economy measures, were in a state of shock.

A *Plain Dealer* editorial, under the heading, "He Says No," acclaimed the Braden performance in these words:

"No,' says James Braden. 'No and no and no!

"A pivotal job, is Braden's, in these days of necessary economies, with the ladle scraping the bottom of the municipal treasury. Some men in office think everyone else should save. Braden thinks they all should.

"The good ship Economy has more conspicuous men in nominal commands; they wear the uniforms and are seen on the bridge. But below decks is Braden with his penchant for saying no when no is the proper answer. Without Braden, or someone with Braden's aptitude with the short monosyllable, the ship, waterlogged as she is, would be in danger of foundering before nightfall.

"Cleveland has reason to be thankful for James Braden. He knows how and when to use the most powerful short word in the English language."

All of which tended to make the Davis aide a standout figure in city administration. But what was not generally known was Braden's hidden ambition, according to Jim Sutphin, one of his young admirers.

"Uncle Jim always fancied himself as something of a lawman, and during this time at City Hall, he got Mayor Davis to win him an appointment as a deputy sheriff. It was a distinction of which he was very proud. He carried the badge with him all the time.

"One day, as he and his wife were riding in the country, a passing motorist almost sideswiped him. Angered, he went after the miscreant and forced him to the side of the road. Both drivers jumped out of their cars and advanced menacingly toward each other. At this point, Braden swung open his suit coat to disclose his deputy sheriff's badge—but the badge, alas, was not there!

"The other driver, meanwhile, continued to advance on Uncle Jim, and when he got close enough, he swung a mighty fist that knocked Uncle Jim to the ground, unconscious. When he woke up, it was to find his head in his wife's lap, and, what really hurt, she was laughing hysterically!"

Jim Braden was at the pinnacle of his second career as the standout in the city administration in 1937 when he decided to fly to Los Angeles. Air travel still had an element of adventure in it, but Jim Braden loved to fly. He took Western Air Express, a forerunner of American Airlines, in a "huge" Boeing transport that carried 13 passengers, including Mr. and Mrs. Martin L. Johnson, world-famous African explorers.

When the plane stopped at Salt Lake City, Braden mailed a postcard to his wife: "Flight very smooth — Rats!" He so loved flying that even the usual turbulence of air travel in that day was something he craved because it added to the excitement of a trip. It was his last communication to his beloved Helen.

The final leg of the trip was from Salt Lake City to Los Angeles

Airport at Burbank. There was foul weather over the San Fernando Valley, with thick fog and heavy rainfall, but the plane had safely cleared the last stretch of mountains, the snowclad range between the Mojave Desert and the San Fernando Valley. On the home stretch, the pilot was unable to pick up the radio directional beam from the Burbank terminal, began

The Cleveland Plain Dealer, Morning edition, January 13, 1937

circling in the fog, and radioed this message: "Coming down to localizer at field." It meant the plane was dropping in altitude in the hope of picking up the radio beam. At that time, the flight was 20 miles northeast of the field, in the foothills of the Tehachapi Mountains.

That was the last message heard by Burbank. At 11:15 a.m., an amateur radio operator reported that he had picked up the faint announcement: "We are coming down in a crash!"

The transport plane hit the ground about 1/2 mile north of the Olive View County Sanitarium in the San Fernando Valley. Patients called out to attendants, reporting that they had heard a terrible crash. Officials put together a large search party that fanned out through the difficult wilderness area. The heavy rain and fog added to the problem, but the rescuers finally came to the site of the disaster. There they found a dozen survivors and the body of Jim Braden. Four of the other passengers, including Martin Johnson, later died of injuries.

The air disaster, and especially the death of Jim Braden, was head-line news. It stunned his many friends back home, especially the members of the Sutphin family, so closely linked to the Bradens through the years. Al Sutphin's first concern was for the welfare of his old friend's widow, Helen. After an interval of mourning, he met with Helen Braden and offered to change the terms by which he had purchased the Braden-Sutphin Ink Company on twenty year terms. Twelve years remained, but Sutphin offered to pay the full amount owed in one payment to Mrs. Braden.

Helen Braden turned down the offer with thanks, insisting that she preferred that the original terms of the contract be observed. Her explanation was that she feared a lump sum payment instead of the monthly check would sever the close ties she enjoyed with the Sutphin family, and she needed that friendship and association now more that ever before.

Jim Braden, appropriately, made one last trip to his beloved island in Canada. He was cremated and his ashes were borne aloft by a bush pilot friend and scattered over Braden's Island.

Helen Braden lived 32 years beyond the death of her husband. She died at age 88 in Cleveland on October 16, 1969. Surviving her were her daughters, Helen Braden Scott and Eleanor Braden Krost. In her last years, Mrs. Braden had taken up residence in the Alcazar Hotel, a neighbor of the Sutphins, who also lived there in later years. The closeness of the two families persisted to the end, and an enduring sign of that warm relationship was the fact that Helen Braden not only was among those who turned a shovel of dirt at the new arena site but carried the title of president of the Braden-Sutphin Ink Company long after Al Sutphin purchase control in 1929; indeed, up to the time of her death 40 years later.

Jim and Helen Braden were symbolically reunited in death. Her ashes also were scattered over Braden's Island in Canada, as her husband's had been so many years before.

The Vulcan Building, the initial home of the Braden Printing Co. (5th floor)

Braden Sutphin Ink match room, circa 1936

Overleaf: Al, the Boxing Commissioner, 1932

CHAPTER SIX

THE TURNING POINT

While he had been active in Cleveland's amateur sports scene for more than a decade, the name Albert C. Sutphin did not find its way into the top headlines of the sports pages of the three Cleveland dailies until he agreed to be the city's boxing and wrestling commissioner in 1932.

Sutphin's acceptance of that post was more an expression of friendship with the recently elected mayor than any wish to play an active role in politics or to become an official part of the fight business. He enjoyed going to the boxing matches, but instinctively he steered clear of the men who managed the business and controlled the fights. As commissioner, of course, he found himself deeply involved. It was a learning experience that he shared with his close friend and brother-in-law, Paul Hoynes, who agreed to serve as a member of the commission at the same time.

Columnist Franklin Porter, extended what amounted to a public expression of sympathy over Sutphin's plight as arbiter of a sport that seemingly was beyond the disciplinary reach of even the highest-minded civic body.

"Albert C. Sutphin is back from Hot Springs," wrote Porter, "where he has been recovering from an overdose of friendship—a friendship which has given him what he suspects is a permanent headache ..."

"Sutphin, a gentleman, an honest man and outstanding sportsman, is chairman of the Cleveland Boxing and Wrestling Commission. He was selected for the post by Mayor Ray T. Miller, whose personal regard for Sutphin is so high that he knew he could not be anything but honest; and Sutphin's loyalty for Miller was so great that he agreed to accept the job.

"Whereupon Sutphin promptly found his hands inserted into the slimy and sordid mess which is professional prizefighting. He learned quickly that many promoters and managers will engage in the most primitive conniving, that his fellow-commissioners are likely to be swayed by strange causes, and that no matter what happens, nothing but grief, misery and commiseration ensues."

By way of example to support this uncomplimentary description of the fight business, the columnist pointed to the first big ring contest to be staged in Cleveland under the supervision of Mayor Miller's newly-appointed fight commission. It featured two nationally-known boxers, Mickey Walker and Johnny Risko; the latter an outstanding Cleveland challenger in the heavyweight division. The contest was to be fought in the newly-opened Cleveland Municipal Stadium.

Sutphin and his fellow-commissioners were on hand for the fight, as were many thousands of fight fans. Exactly how many became the issue of the night. Sports announcer Tom Manning told his radio audience that there were 35,000 customers in the stadium, which brought a frown to Sutphin's face in light of the turnstile count of just over 10,000.

Al Sutphin always had a good eye for the size of a crowd, and his sizeup of the gate was that it was a lot closer to Manning's 35,000 than it was to the official count of 10,000. The distressed fight promoter, Tommy McGinty, saw the larger estimate as closer to the truth also.

"Investigation later proved that someone in power had stood near a small side door and 'passed' his friends into the show," wrote Porter. "Sutphin is still wondering how several thousand were able to sneak through that tiny gate."

Whitey Lewis of the Press, gave it as his blunt estimate that 15,000 persons were "hustled into the joint by political shills ..."

Moving to clean up the situation, Sutphin saw to it that the commission he headed became affiliated with the National Boxing Association, leading Porter to comment that, thanks to Sutphin, the fight business in Cleveland had become "as clean as it had been in years."

"Then the storm broke," he wrote. "In Akron, one Willie (Gorilla) Jones held the N.B.A. middleweight title. In New York, Ben Jeby held the New York Boxing Commission's world title. Experts thought that Jones could beat Jeby with one hand, and a match was made here (Cleveland) to find out.

"On one condition would Hymie Caplan, manager of Jeby, do business with Suey Welch, manager of Jones. Neither title would be at

Ben Jeby

Gorilla Jones

take. To do this, both fighters had to come into the ring above the weight limit of 160 pounds.

"Well, they had the weighing-in and Jones, who was in fair condition, knew that he couldn't make better than 150 pounds. He donned a large pair of shoes and attempted to insert a few pounds of scrap iron between the soles. Sutphin saw it.

"He thought quickly. His instincts were to make the fighters weigh. If he did, however, Jeby would not have fought and the city would have lost much revenue from Public Hall. Sutphin closed his eyes. Friendship counted. The fight with all its later explosions (the men were thrown out for stalling) went ahead.

"Those two incidents ought to give a pretty fair picture of the position in which this gentleman sportsman finds himself. For the sake of the mayor, he and his friend Hoynes will carry on ..."

However distasteful this experience undoubtedly was, Sutphin's day in the public limelight was valuable in making him known to Clevelanders who might never have heard of him except as the ink salesman with the red tie. The flaming cravat was a personal idiosyncrasy of the Champ, his badge of identity among his friends and clients in the ink business. It had not been a calculated attention-getter in the beginning; simply the outgrowth of a gag that he had encountered in the Graphic Arts Bowling League, of which he had been secretary for over twenty years. The bowlers traditionally wore red neckties on their banquet night, and Sutphin liked the idea so much that he began to wear vivid neckwear all the time. It inevitably became the Sutphin trademark.

Columnist Polly Parsons, in a piece devoted to the Champ, told her readers that, "You'll recognize Al Sutphin by the red neckties—unless it's St. Patrick's Day, and then the necktie will be green, but violent green. Red neckties sell red ink, black ink, gold ink, and every known color and shade of ink. The Braden-Sutphin Company has a quarter-million formulas."

Parsons recalled an incident in which Sutphin met with an important banker during his drive to enlist financing for the hockey arena. Awed by the prospect of meeting such a highly-placed executive, Sutphin substituted a conservative dark necktie for the usual red one.

"The first words the banker said to him were: 'I heard you always wore red neckties, but I see you don't.'" He was obviously disappointed.

Sutphin never made that mistake again. People had come to expect him to wear red ties, and from that time on, he never let them down.

When Jim Sutphin, the older of his two sons, followed in Al's footsteps as a salesman for the ink company, he had an experience in his travels which pointed up the power of his father's trademark. It came about in a visit to the Salem Label Company in Salem, Ohio.

"So you're the son of Al Sutphin!", exclaimed a female executive of the company. "He used to call on our company many years ago. I always felt kind of sorry for him."

"Why?", asked the puzzled Jim. He had never known anyone who felt sorry for his father.

"Well," she said, "every time he came in here, he wore a red tie, and I thought at the time, 'Gee! The poor guy can't afford but one tie!'"

Jim never forgot that incident. He didn't have the heart to tell her the truth.

"Little did she realize that Dad used to buy 144 red ties—a whole gross—at a time. He always wore a new tie. He never got them dry cleaned. When a tie got stained or dirty, he would just throw it away. It was also his habit to give red ties to friends and acquaintances, not to mention strangers. He gave away hundreds of red ties in a year's time."

So it was that the vivid red tie became a personal insignia that Clevelanders came to recognize as part of the Sutphin persona.

Mary & Al "clowning" with Whitey Lewis and his wife

Sutphin's luncheon meeting with Whitey Lewis in 1932 was a turning point in his life. Lewis was sincere enough that day in urging the little-known executive to give up his post on the boxing and wrestling commission, but he had a double objective in mind. Hockey was one of his favorite sports and he had the hope that Sutphin would be the one to rescue the faltering Falcons, Cleveland's entry in the International Hockey League.

Harry (Hap) Holmes, owner of the franchise, had reached the end of his financial tether after three years of a money-losing attempt to interest Clevelanders in the professional sport, and the franchise was about to go down the drain.

Ice hockey was a relatively new sport in the American scheme of things. It had come down through Canada and made its first appearance in Cleveland in 1890, when it became a fairly popular, amateur team sport. The first professional ice hockey team in Cleveland did not arrive on the scene until Holmes took the gamble in 1929.

Whitey Lewis was not only a highly competent journalist, he was also articulate, intelligent and personable. Al Sutphin liked Lewis, just as, in fact, he liked most journalists. They were, after all, part of the print business and could be regarded in that respect as brothers under the skin.

Lewis was a shrewd judge of character who admired Al Sutphin as one of the standouts in sports. In that luncheon meeting he pointedly played to Sutphin's weakness for all kinds of athletic activity, with special emphasis on hockey. Sutphin's weakness was also one of his strengths. Hockey was a game he had enjoyed playing as a youngster on ice ponds in the park and on the rink with the Central High team. He knew it to be a game with enough spectacle to sell itself to Clevelanders.

There was an inherent challenge in the newspaperman's suggestion that he take over a failing hockey team, and it appealed to his salesman's pride. Sutphin was a realist who recognized that Hap Holmes' Falcons had no future so long as they were restricted by the limitations imposed on the team by its home rink. The Elysium could not accommodate more than 2,000 patrons and that was not enough to support a professional team.

Buying the Cleveland Falcons would be a relatively easy, low-price investment, he knew. But to make the team financially and artistically successful would be a major undertaking that would demand as a primary requisite the construction of a large, expensive new ice rink. A new arena.

Sutphin didn't hesitate in making his decision. Lewis had made an accurate judgment. The challenge that he had laid before the Champ was one that he could not refuse. A new era in Cleveland sports was about to begin.

Al signs the final contract for the Arena

Whitey Lewis speaks at the Arena groundbreaking ceremony

Overleaf: Groundbreaking for the Arena, May 8, 1937

CHAPTER SEVEN

SUTPHIN'S SURPRISE

The same kind of civic excitement that Cleveland was to experience more than a half-century later with the building of the Gateway sports complex downtown was generated in the middle-1930s by the planning, financing and construction of Al Sutphin's big new Arena on Euclid Avenue.

The Arena was one of two major ventures that gave the city a lift in spirits at that crucial time in its history. The other was the Great Lakes Exposition, a lakefront fair that was a combination of a carnival, a cultural show and an amusement park. It enjoyed a two-year run.

Everyone who has attempted to describe the Great Depression adequately has faltered in the effort because the words come together generally as so much hyperbole within the context of today's reality. It was a terrible time of joblessness, deflation, stagnation, pessimism and hopelessness.

Cleveland, more than most American cities of the time, was deep in the doldrums. What made the situation here more grievous was that Cleveland had experienced nothing but success in its years of incredible growth from the 1850's through 1930. It was a boomtown during those 80 years; the breeding place of great industry and new fortunes. Of the 68 millionaires named in the New York Tribune's 1892 list of America's richest people, 53 were Clevelanders.

The city's reversal of fortunes was in shocking contrast with its cocky, winning past. Morale did not decline, it plummeted. The city was at a standstill. Not a single new building of any size was under construction, nor contemplated, in 1935.

It may have been the worst time in history for a newcomer to professional sports to think about building a large facility as costly as an ice arena, but Sutphin walked where others feared to tread. He went to the banking interests—those that had survived the national bank holiday of 1933—and laid out his building plans in his bid for financial support.

The bankers, benumbed by all that happened to crush the economy in a few years, were polite and sympathetic in their discussions with Sutphin, but they were blunt in pointing out the foolhardiness of an Arena venture. They turned him down.

In truth, common sense seemed to be on the side of the bankers. The need for a professional sports facility had to be questioned. Professional sports events in general were relatively low-key affairs in the early decades of the century. The leading pro sports were boxing and baseball. Football did not establish itself as a pay-for-play sport until the late 1940's, and then only after repeated attempts and failures. Basketball did not win a foothold on the professional sports scene until that same post-war era.

While professional ice hockey had been introduced to Cleveland in 1929, it was no more than a minor attraction, and certainly a clear failure on the financial side. The Cleveland team's shortcomings were quite clear. It was a minor league club stocked with ordinary talent, playing a foreign game in a wholly inadequate ice rink.

On the plus side, Al Sutphin was a successful businessman. More important, perhaps, was his record as an outstanding salesman. But his talent and background could not overcome the basic disadvantages perceived by the bankers. They probably would have refused to lend money for a new arena even in normal economic times. The conventional wisdom held that a sports arena was an unwise investment, and they brought forth some telling statistics to bolster their argument. Quite apart from the somber fact that the depression had deprived most Americans of recreational spending money, there was also the dismaying fact that sports facilities generally were single-purpose buildings, seasonal in nature and doomed to be dark and vacant during many months of the year.

A conspicuous example, only a few years old, was the mammoth Cleveland Municipal Stadium.

Built primarily as a home for Indians baseball, it went virtually unused—except for a rare, special game—from the time of its grand opening in 1933 until Bill Veeck bought the team in 1946 and transferred the Indians' home games from old League Park to the downtown amphitheater a year later. If the long baseball season could not put Cleveland

Stadium in the black, the relatively short hockey schedule would not be enough to make a new arena pay for itself.

Sutphin knew this to be true. He was not blind to the financial facts of sports life. Few men, including the bankers, could represent themselves as being as knowledgeable about sports arenas as he was.

Cleveland Stadium (1933)

Sutphin had made a national survey of such facilities before deciding to go ahead with the project. He had reviewed individual arena records, visited with the owners, drawn on their successes and failures. In the end he came to the educated conclusion that a new arena could be a successful enterprise in Cleveland.

What the hockey promoter relied on in going counter to the advice of the experts was mainly confidence in himself and the mode of operation that he had in mind. He envisioned much more than a hockey rink. What he contemplated was a facility designed as an all-purpose building, a center for many types of entertainment and public functions. Sutphin's arena would be ablaze with lights year-round, with a full schedule of hockey, ice shows, boxing, wrestling, dances, high school and college basketball, track meets and exhibitions of all kinds. In short, Sutphin proposed a state-of-the-art, sports, entertainment and civic center, unmatched by any complex west of Madison Square Garden.

"That kind of an arena," said the man from the ink company, "will pay for itself."

In the main, onlookers in the business and banking community, as well as the Cleveland sports writers, kept at a respectful distance. The city wanted Sutphin's dream to come true, but there was a skepticism born of many disappointments.

"On your ink company,' the financial wizards said, 'we will lend you our shirts. On a sports arena, not a dime!'

"'I'll fool 'em,' said Sutphin to himself. 'I'll finance it myself.'"

What followed was a marketing *tour de force*; a demonstration of skating on thin financial ice worthy of an Olympic gold medal.

Al Sutphin set off on an unrelenting promotional crusade in which he gently, but forcibly, prodded friends, associates, advertisers, sports fans, civic leaders, passersby—everyone he thought might be a prospect—into investing in his arena.

The same kind of civic excitement that Cleveland was to experience more than a half-century later with the Gateway complex was generated in 1937 by Al Sutphin's daring project. Gateway was undeniably more elaborate in scope, but in its time, the Arena was a comparable undertaking.

There was one very important difference. To accomplish Gateway, supporters looked to the taxpayers to provide hundreds of millions of dollars of financing in the form of direct costs, abatements and concessions carrying far into the next century. The Arena looked to Al Sutphin.

The Arena was privately planned and privately financed. It tapped no public funds, required no taxes, involved no public agencies, and received no abatements, concessions or contributions from the public sector.

The final cost of the Arena, converted to 1995 dollars, represents the modern equivalent of over $20,000,000. Except for one insurance company loan, the money came from individual investors. Prominent among them was Al Sutphin himself and most of his friends and business associates.

The success of the Arena fund-raising was a dramatic demonstration of faith in the Champ's personal integrity and vision by his fellow Clevelanders. The building that materialized out of his dream reflected their good judgment.

The Champ kept reminding investors that what he was about to build was not simply an ice rink for a hockey team, but a year-around entertainment center with a stabilizing anchor of shops and offices. Dancing this concept in the eyes of business prospects, he sold long-term leases to desirable tenants, including the American Legion, the W. F. Ryan Insurance Company, Cleveland Sports Goods and the Ohio Sports Service Company.

Once interior space in the building had been sold, he went about the task of selling wall space in the lobby and within the great amphitheater itself. Clients who were persuaded by Sutphin to come into the Arena fold included the Ford Motor Company, Bond Clothes, Spencerian Schools, Richman Brothers Clothes, Hitz Hotels, Fisher Foods, Cleveland Ice Cream, Sutcliffe Studios, and Alfred John Skates. The income from these leases totaled almost enough to pay the ongoing costs of the building.

Sutphin's creativity was stretched to the limit as he hunted out every possible source of revenue. One of his more extreme ideas—and one of the few that never came to fruition—was his proposal to an Akron rubber company that, in exchange for a 10-year contract at $60,000 a year, he would build the Arena's entrance in the form of an enormous automobile tire bearing the manufacture's name, promising that every ticket sold would carry the company name. In his zeal to fund his project, Sutphin had come up with the concept of "naming rights" fifty years ahead of its time. But the company turned him down.

"Why, Mr. Sutphin, people may not even be riding on rubber tires ten years from now," a company executive said, demonstrating less faith in his own products that he had in the Champ's Arena.

Other unique commercial tie-ins that the Champ devised for sale met with rejection, causing him to ponder the limited imagination of big business. Among the ill-fated ideas were proposals to build the Arena front in the form of a gigantic gas station, a monster soup can and a cornucopian grocery store.

"I learned a lot about gasoline and soup and groceries," he said, "but I didn't get my leases."

Acknowledging that he would have to concentrate on smaller advertisers for the revenue needed, Sutphin the Salesman went to work in earnest. What he needed was contractual agreements with enough of those small advertisers to guarantee the $60,000 annual payment on the Arena loan debt, and he achieved that goal in 18 months. During that time of quiet salesmanship, he had to endure some jibes from sports writers who wondered in print if the Arena project had been nothing but the idle speculation of a starry-eyed promoter.

Once he had lined up enough advertisers to assure that there would be enough revenue on hand to make the annual loan payments, Sutphin turned to the next stage—selling enough stock to bring in $500,000. This was the purely personal phase of his money-raising campaign as he went from one acquaintance to another, asking for each to invest in his dream. The response was remarkable.

"Faith built the Arena," columnist Ed McAuley wrote later. "The hockey club, so far as the average investor was concerned, wasn't worth more than its old uniforms would bring at auction. Al Sutphin's word was priceless. He asked his friends to invest a half million in his dream. He didn't have to ask them twice."

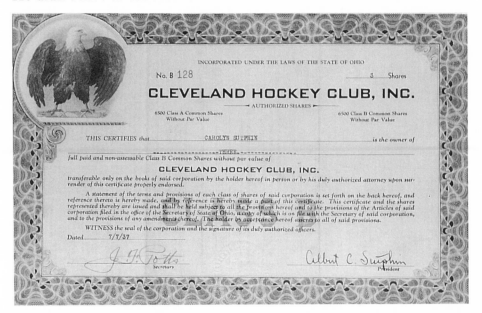

Cleveland Arena stock certificate

A Cleveland banker told McAuley, "I've never seen anything to equal what Sutphin has done. People I didn't think had a nickel have raised from $1,500 to $15,000 to put in his Arena. When I ask them about it, they simply say, 'Al Sutphin's behind it. That's enough for me.'"

In some instances it was a case of salesmanship in reverse as some of Al's friends insisted on investing in spite of his reluctance to put them at risk, knowing how meager their resources were. One was Al's regular barber, whose finances were not far from the subsistence level. He had such faith in Al that he brushed aside arguments that it would be unwise to dabble in such a speculative project. Even as Sutphin was making his negative points, the barber went to his cash register and pulled a $100 bill out from under the cash drawer, tucked away for a rainy day.

"Take this," ordered the barber, handing the money to Sutphin. "If anyone can make a go of this Arena thing, Albert, you can!"

Sutphin's sales effort was helped tremendously by his own rise in prominence. All of his activity in behalf of amateur sports through the years, as Mayor Miller's commissioner, the laudatory columns about him as the owner of the Cleveland Falcons and the Elysium, his and his popularity —all gave his Arena sales an integrity that made his eloquence credible.

An indication of the high regard in which Sutphin was held by Clevelanders was manifest in January, 1936, when a testimonial dinner

Al's Night at the Mayfair

in his honor was sponsored "by his host of friends" at a brand-new Cleveland institution that already was receiving national publicity.

The Mayfair Casino was as elaborate as any supper club in America and the forerunner of the casinos that would sprout up in Las Vegas. It had risen from the stripped-down Ohio Theater in Playhouse Square; a huge nightclub made possible by the disastrous fall-off in theater patronage caused by the depression.

More than 700 people filled the Mayfair that night to do honor to Al Sutphin. They came from all parts of the U. S. and Canada and included printers, lithographers, ink-makers, hockey players and officials, baseball moguls, lion tamers, Rotarians, golfers, war veterans, and a large political delegation headed by the Mayor Harold H. Burton. (Burton would go on to become a U. S. Senator and Associate Justice of the Supreme Court.)

As large as the Mayfair Casino was, it could not accommodate all those who wanted to show their appreciation of Al Sutphin. Tickets were sold out days in advance. Each guest was given a red necktie to wear, and the Champ's profile was silhouetted on the program with the extra large bowl pipe stuck in his mouth.

The final touch of the testimonial program, after a series of laudatory speeches, was given by a former wartime buddy who sang Al's favorite song: "Find Me a Four Leaf Clover".

An ink industry trade magazine described the evening in these words:

"To say Al was surprised would be putting it mildly. The only tip-off he had was that there was going to be a small craftsmen's gathering...

"First, the Mayor openly paid his respects to Al Sutphin as a leading citizen of the City of Cleveland. This was a real compliment...because Al had supported the opposing candidate.

"Then Al was toasted as a businessman, hockey magnate, a friend and a citizen. As a finale, he was presented with a trophy.

"The humor of the evening was furnished by Al himself, who by the time he was called upon, had become sufficiently composed to be himself. The prize line of his speech, in referring to the fact that printers had paid to come to the dinner, was "when printers have anything to do with me, it costs them money!"

"After the dinner, the guests were entertained with the Mayfair Casino show, which closed with the chorus marching across the stage spelling out Al's name. Then the guests were motored to the Elysium Ice Rink....And as a fit conclusion to the evening, the Cleveland hockey team won."

The syndicate of investors that eventually came together to finance the Arena was led by Sutphin and Carl F. Lezius, a friend of long standing. It included other friends: Ellis R. Ryan, F.J. Potts, and Hap Holmes. The financing to cover the original cost was spread out among many Clevelanders, but the important base was a loan from Union Central Life Insurance Company of Cincinnati. The remainder was $650,000 of debentures in $100 denominations, each purchased by some 300 investors. Each debenture carried one share of common stock. Sutphin, Lezius and their families, the associates and employees of the Braden-Sutphin Ink Company, and the Leizius-Hiles Printing Company altogether bought $200,000 worth of debentures.

Sutphin's 25-years in the printing business had won him many friends in the industry and they rallied unhesitatingly to his side in the

Arena campaign. Those same investors were well represented among the officers and directors of Cleveland Hockey, Inc.

Thirteen thousand shares of common stock were issued; 6,500 of which went with the debentures and the remainder to the promoters. Sutphin and Lezius, the two leaders of the enterprise, would not be allowed promotion expenses or lease commissions, nor even, in the beginning, salaries to cover their time and effort and talent. Only when the debentures were paid off did they begin sharing equally with the other stockholders in the profits.

Ellis Ryan   *Albert C. Sutphin*   *Carl F. Lezius*

Paul Hoynes   *Don Robinson*   *T.J. Conway*   *Frank Conat*   *J.A. Gideon*

Board of Directors
The Arena

(not all directors are shown)

O.M. Garber   *G.L. Erikson*   *Fred Danner*   *C.E. Sutphen*

"It has been a hobby with us," said Carl Lezius. "Eighty percent of this venture has been Al's work, and 20 percent of it mine."

"Then I had to sell hockey," Al Sutphin recalled. "The Barons had been playing in the Elysium, with a seating capacity of 1,900, and so far as I knew, no more than 1,900 people in Cleveland ever had seen a hockey game. I had to dig up 8,000 more to fill the Arena. I had to sell hockey to people who didn't know what they were buying..."

In the beginning, all Sutphin had for an asset was the old Cleveland Hockey Club, which wasn't nearly as old as it was weak. Harry (Hap)

Holmes' organization had turned over to Sutphin such assets as it could count as its own. They included the team itself (the faltering Falcons), the Elysium rink and the land beneath it, the International Hockey League

"Hap" Holmes

franchise, and the club's books, which offered only a deficit.

A Falcons asset which was acquired by Sutphin was Harry Holmes himself. He agreed to become an officer of the reorganized club on a no-pay basis, as an assistant to Carl F. Lezius. It was appropriate that Sutphin should have rewarded Holmes with an active role in his expanding organization. He was the pioneer enthusiast who had done more to acquaint Clevelanders with the game of ice hockey than any other person. He had learned, as most pioneers do, that there

is a painful price to pay for being the first to try to sell a new idea..

Hap (short for "Happy") Holmes was a native of Ontario who had won his nickname because of his ready smile and good nature. He was an outstanding hockey player himself. In 1910, as an amateur in Toronto, he played on four championships in hockey, lacrosse, football and softball, all in the same year. He turned professional with Toronto in 1911, played on a championship team in 1913 and then moved to a team in Seattle which won the title in 1916 and 1918. His appearance in a total of 32 Stanley Cup games is still in the record books.

At the age of 38, this veteran goal tender joined the Detroit Red Wings. He shut out the opposing teams in 13 of the last 18 games he played, finally retiring from active play at the age of 40.

Al Sutphin admired quality as a hockey fan and as a businessman, and he found both in Hap Holmes. He counted the former owner of the Falcons as perhaps the most valuable asset to be transferred in his acquisition of the failing club.

The site chosen for the new Arena was a large tract of land on Euclid Avenue, near E. 40th Street, close to the eastern edge of what had been, only a few decades earlier, one of the world's most fashionable boulevards. Sutphin purchased the former estate of Charles F. Brush, the famous inventor of the electric arc light, who had made history with the first outdoor demonstration of electric illumination on Cleveland's

Public Square on April 29, 1879. The address was 3700 Euclid Avenue. Only a few hundred yards away was the former home of the world's richest man, John D. Rockefeller.

The Brush estate extended from Euclid Avenue on the south to Chester Avenue on the north. Close to Chester was an enormous windmill which had been used by the inventor in his power generator experiments.

Franz Warner
Architect

The great stone mansion facing the avenue that the Brush family had called home had fallen victim to the times like so many other magnificent residences on Euclid Avenue's world-renowned "Millionaires' Row."

It was an impressive piece of real estate, measuring 265 feet frontage on Euclid Avenue and 572 feet from Euclid to Chester Avenue. A clause in the Brush will provided that the site never be sold or leased to anyone who might use the property for "rooming houses or the like." The inventor obviously feared that his home would share the sad fate of so many of the great houses along the avenue. The mansion was torn down shortly after the death of its owner.

It was bargain basement time for real estate in Cleveland in 1936 and Sutphin bought the Brush property for a tiny fraction of its worth, estimated at a million dollars. By 1936, its tax valuation had dropped to $149,160, but the price paid by Sutphin was reported at $75,000.

The plan was for the Arena to front on Euclid Avenue. Franz Warner of the architectural firm of Warner & Mitchell designed the huge building, 265 feet wide by 329 feet deep.

Another large building on the Chester Avenue side would house the Braden-Sutphin Ink Company, linked to the Arena by underground passageway. The ink plant was Sutphin's way of combining his business interests. The new Arena needed construction capital. The ink company needed larger quarters. So Sutphin sold himself a lease for a new ink factory and office building on the land owned by the Arena. The left hand did know what the right hand was doing.

Ground was broken for the new Arena on May 8, 1937, and some of the city's more cynical sportswriters and editorialists hastened to make amends for past expressions of disbelief with a torrent of adjectives praising Sutphin and all of his investors.

Work was begun immediately by the construction company, Gillmore, Charmichael & Olson under Sutphin's demanding schedule for completion by year's end. Whether it was because of the Champ's deadline or simply the novelty of such a large construction project in the middle of the depression, the work proceeded at a fast pace. Only six months and two days passed from the date of groundbreaking to the opening of the Arena to the public on November 10, 1937!

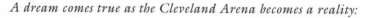

A dream comes true as the Cleveland Arena becomes a reality:

...the Arena in progress

To appreciate this accomplishment, a comparison of the Arena with the mammoth Cleveland Public Hall (four years in the making) shows the Arena to be 50 feet longer and 100 feet wider in its measurement of 329 feet by 264 feet.

As the new building neared completion, Sutphin called together a group of Cleveland sports writers and invited them to suggest an appropriate name for the new structure. Their choice, without argument, was "The Arena."

Still in the christening mode, Sutphin announced that the Cleveland public would be given the privilege of investing his hockey team with a new name. He felt the club ought to move into its splendid new home with a fresh identity. The Cleveland Hockey Club, the formal corporate name of the Sutphin enterprise, offered $1,000 in cash prizes

The future begins to take shape

to the winners of a newspaper contest to name the franchise. The sum would be split in two parts, with a grand prize of $500 going to the person submitting the name chosen by the judges. The winner was Clevelander Joseph Tocca who came up with the memorable moniker, the "Cleveland Barons."

The final touches

Cleveland Arena (1937)

Thanks to Architect Franz Warner and his masterful interpretation of Al Sutphin's dream, the Barons would skate onto the ice of one of the most beautiful sports facilities in America. Warner had proceeded on his design only after a study of two of the most famous rinks in Canada, the Maple Leaf Gardens in Toronto and the Montreal Forum, incorporating the best features of each in his blueprint for Cleveland.

Cleveland Arena (Interior)

The interior of the building had a stunning impact on first-time customers. Warner had incorporated beauty into the utilitarian requirements, and the Sutphin influence was plainly apparent in the bold use of

The Great Clock

color. The 10,000 seats were divided into three sections of different colors—red, white and blue. The ticket colors corresponded to each of the three sections, making it easy for customers to find their seat.

Another customer-friendly element was the open nature of the interior design. Despite the Arena's enormous size, only four steel piers were used to support the network of steel below roof, held in position by four of the largest cross beams in the world.

The base of the Arena floor was concrete, covered with 4-inch insulation and zinc plates, supporting a grid of refrigeration pipes buried in concrete and terrazzo. The top section, covered by frozen water, formed a field for ice hockey games and shows like the Ice Follies and was easily converted to solid flooring for dancing, basketball, expositions, boxing and wrestling, and other uses.

The seating capacity for hockey games was 9,600 and escalated to 15,000 for attractions that allowed floor seating, like boxing.

A conspicuous feature of the interior auditorium was a great clock that hung from the roof over the center of the auditorium. It was a multi-purpose chronometer with a conventional clock face that also served as an official stop watch, clicking off the time in seconds and minutes for sports contests.

The ice rink itself was floodlighted with a battery of 1500-watt bulbs and a backup of 20 searchlights when needed, as well as the usual theatrical flood-lights and spotlights. Press and radio booths were at high vantage points at opposing ends of the rink. In addition to many concession stands, the Arena sported a huge bierstube, or rathskellar, almost 200 feet long and half as deep. It was an abstraction calculated to make the most despondent hockey fan forget a night's defeat.

One thing was made certain by the new Arena. The hockey team that represented Cleveland may have been minor league in its classification, but henceforth it would play in a major league setting.

There were two lobbies. A North Lobby measured 128 by 46 feet and featured the Pilsner Bavarian Village. The South Lobby measured 56 by 54 feet. The customers had plenty of room to mill around in, quaff beer, hot dogs and wiener schnitzel.

The Barvarian Village

A unique feature of the Arena construction was the placement of the ice rink surface itself below ground level, an approach that reduced costs considerably. It was the only arena in the United States so constructed at that time.

The extent of the construction effort can best be appreciated with a review of the statistics so lovingly compiled by the Sutphin office. It was necessary, for example, for the builder to excavate 35,000 cubic yards of soil to get the necessary "bowl effect." The construction company had to use 1,200 tons of structural steel, 14,000 barrels of cement, and 700,000 bricks that weighed, altogether, 2,500 tons.

That such a massive building, with all its inner refinements, could have been built in six months, from start to finish, staggers the imagination. But that was the actual timetable of the Arena, and there can't be any doubt that Al Sutphin was ever present in the background, urging the workers to greater effort. He was an impatient man.

The Brush Mansion, circa 1934

The vacant lot at 3701 Euclid Avenue, April, 1937

Overleaf: The Arena

CHAPTER EIGHT

THE FUTURE IS NOW

It was a climactic moment for Al Sutphin when his creation, that grand building called the Arena, had its ceremonial opening against the background of a cheering city in the autumn of 1937.

The only glitch in the proceedings was a fire in the small frame building across the street which had served as temporary office of the hockey club. Sutphin was notified of the blaze while hosting a civic banquet, and he rushed off to the scene in his evening clothes. Although the damages were slight in terms of money—an estimated $300—the most serious loss was the irreplaceable records of the hockey club. In all the confusion at the scene, Sutphin calmly announced to reporters that the sale of tickets for the inaugural Arena events would begin the following Friday at the temporary box office at 3716 Euclid Avenue. It was a grand show of aplomb.

While the incident had a temporary shock effect, it had no influence on the scheduled grand opening program: three weeks of events beginning with a musical extravaganza, *The Ice Follies of 1938.*

The first hockey game would be an exhibition contest between the Cleveland Barons and the New York Rangers, champions of the National Hockey League, on November 17th. The Barons would play the Syracuse Stars in the regular International-American League season opener three days later.

Some 8,000 guests were on hand for the formal baptism of the Arena on November 10th, the opening night of the Ice Follies. That performance was preceded by a short, emotional speaking program in which some of the celebrities on hand praised BOTH the building and Al Sutphin. Mayor Burton acclaimed "the fighting heart of Al Sutphin" as the force behind the new Cleveland sports facility. Senator Robert Bulkley spoke in like terms. In his brief reply, Sutphin's voice broke with emotion of the moment as he recalled the years of struggle that had gone into the project.

"I begged and pleaded with my friends to put money into this arena," he recalled, "but I thought tonight I would offer an apology for

Opening night at the Arena

working so hard on them. But I guess I did them a favor by taking them away from the stock market."

His voice grew stronger and took on a ring of pride as he introduced those who were his associates in the venture and briefly sketched their contributions and the obstacles that had been surmounted.

"In light of what we went through," he said, "you will understand why we nicknamed this building 'Aspirin Plaza.'"

The crowd roared and applauded the down-to-earth remarks of the man who had given them reason to be cheerful.

Windsor French was present and provided his usual sharp observations in his *Cleveland Press* column.

"Senator Bulkley and Mayor Burton, among other dignitaries," he noted, "were widely separated in their respective boxes, one gathers, not for political reasons, but to give Announcer Red Manning an opportunity to exploit his ability as he glided about, microphone in hand, a carrot-haired Hans Brinker on a bright new pair of silver skates.

"The celebrities made speeches. Mr. Sutphin offered his various votes of thanks, and Red Manning scattered adjectives until the air was heavy with them. I suppose it should be mentioned also that the hall is vast, handsome and comfortable ..."

The Arena ice mosaic

John Dietrich, who covered hockey for the *Plain Dealer*, was a glowering presence in that newspaper's sports department, but the new Arena broke through his usual reserve.

"To the fans of Cleveland, who have been waiting years and years for this spot, "he wrote, "it can be said that the Arena is gorgeous. Sutphin apparently hasn't forgotten a thing."

The headlines of Bob Godley's review of the Arena opener in *The Press* was typical of the exuberance of the fourth estate:

BEST IN WORLD: THAT'S NEW SPORTS PALACE HERE

Perhaps the most unusual of the newspaper reviews of the Arena on its opening night came from the *Plain Dealer's* drama critic, William F McDermott, a nationally respected student of the theater who had covered thousands of first night affairs. He wrote:

"... The new Arena is startling. It surrounds a primitive art with luxury. It adds comfort to what was once ascetic. It makes an elaborate and sensuous spectacle of a primitive art.

"Even the appearance of the ice is immeasurably changed. The spacious expanse of smooth ice in the new Arena is laid out in a mosaic pattern of rich and lively colors centered with a great circle, in a multi-colored peacock design. It looks like an inlaid mosaic floor of fine tile in some incredibly vast luxurious Moorish palace.

The Ice Follies

"A stage producer such as Florenz Ziegfeld would be enraptured by the possibilities of the Arena for the presentation of magnificent spectacles. All the pictorial grace that he strove for, all the opulence and originality of effect that he lived for, would be made easier and multiplied if he could have put his silken beauties on skates.

"This new ice-skating Arena is not only an important addition to the recreational assets of the town. It may also be the beginning of a new kind of theatrical art."

Newspapers in other cities took notice and there was an envious tone in their stories. A Buffalo newspaper commented:

"Buffalo is without a hockey rink except the one now under course of construction at Nichols School for its own exclusive use.

"Cleveland has one, recently constructed near the downtown section. We might add that Cleveland has an Al Sutphin. We haven't..."

The *New York World-Telegram*, reporting the game between the Barons and the New York Rangers, described the new Cleveland Arena as "just about the last word in sportive structures."

"You can take it as official that Cleveland won't be in the minors more than this season. The club now possesses one of the finest rinks in the United States and the magnates figure to grab the (Montreal) Maroons and NHL franchise for the 1938-39 campaign.

"Bill" Cook

"When Sutphin wants something," the *World-Telegram* piece concluded, "he shells out for it in a large way. Bill Cook is receiving the highest minor league salary in the history of hockey."

A few nights later, when the Cook-coached Barons trounced the Syracuse Stars in their first league game in the Arena, Sutphin was asked if he might be inclined to tear up Cook's two-year contract and improve the terms.

"What contract?" Sutphin asked. "Bill has no contract. My word is just as good as any contract, and so is Cook's, and we have an understanding that, by mutual consent, he will remain here for at least two years."

The Cleveland team that took to the ice in that event-filled autumn of 1937 was as new as the arena itself. It was a wholly different squad of players than the one that had finished in third place the previous season. Sutphin was realist enough to know that an attractive, comfortable setting was only part of the success formula. The team itself had to be good enough to draw fans into the Arena on a regular basis. The product had to meet the same high standards of quality as its gleaming new facility.

One of Sutphin's most important moves was hiring the living legend, Cook, as the new coach of the Barons. Cook had starred for the New York Rangers for 12 years, averaging 40 points a season for a career total of 450 points. His active career as a player reached back more than a quarter-century, but he was evasive on the subject of age. Official sources estimated him to be 40 or 41, but even those guesses amused all the NHL players who were sure he was older.

Age didn't matter in the case of Bill Cook. He was one of the greatest players the game ever had known, still outstanding at the time of his retirement in 1937. The Ranger forward line of Bill Cook, Frank Boucher, and Fred (Bun) Cook, Bill's brother, may have been the best ever. Adding to the Cook family aura of greatness was a third brother, Alex, known more familiarly as Bud. Eventually all three would be drawn into the Barons' fold by Sutphin.

The Cleveland Barons (1937)

When he began his search for a new coach, Sutphin naturally alighted on Cook's name. He consulted Les Patrick, general manager of the New York Rangers, who supported Cook as the best possible choice. But Patrick made Sutphin promise never to interfere with Cook as coach. Sutphin agreed.

When Patrick was in Cleveland for the grand opening of the Arena, he had a reunion with his former star player and took the opportunity to ask him, jokingly, if Sutphin were holding to his promise not to interfere.

"Interfere?" exclaimed Cook. "Hell, he doesn't even speak to me!"

The new coach was exaggerating, but it was an important point. It was Sutphin's style, in the ink sales business or in sports, to give an employee the latitude to carry out his job successfully. The relationship between Bill Cook and Al Sutphin quickly went beyond any business arrangement. They became the closest of friends for many years and the whole Sutphin family shared in the relationship by spending summer vacations in Kingston, Ontario, close to the Cooks.

The Cleveland hockey sextet that took the ice in the 1937-38 season under Bill Cook bore little resemblance to the Falcons. It was a new team with a new name, a new coach, and, of course, a new arena. The city responded with record attendance figures.

If there was anything controversial about the reborn Cleveland hockey team, it was the name of the 'Barons.' Several of the sports columnists ridiculed the name, with one wondering out loud if the team would be "baron of talent" and "baron of victories."

Sutphin shrugged off the criticism good-humoredly.

"When you get fifteen hundred letters telling you how lousy the name is," he argued, "and when it's thrown at you in every club, it's the best you could get."

The exhibition match with the New York Rangers was preceded by a dinner in the Arena's north lobby attended by some 300 sports writers, radio broadcasters, friends of Al Sutphin, and representatives of other cities who were interested in the new Arena as a possible model for their own communities. Among the speakers were NHL President Calder, after whom the minor league championship cup was named. Calder said he had been hearing of a new arena in Cleveland "for at least ten years," and had come to the city as far back as 1926 to look over a proposed site. At that time, he said, the unnamed promoters had concluded a new ice rink in Cleveland was absolutely impossible.

"I have helped Mr. Sutphin realize one of his ambitions," said Calder. "Now I hope that he will help me realize one of my ambitions. I want to see a National League franchise in Cleveland!"

Calder had good reason to speak of a future Cleveland franchise in the NHL. Bill Cook's Barons had gotten off on a season start so hot it should have melted the American-International League ice. The Barons' attendance and box office receipts also gripped the attention of all the NHL arena owners. In seven games played, the Barons had drawn 48,000 customers.

It was estimated that the Barons would draw about 148,000 customers in the 1937-38 season in their new home.
As it turned out, about 250,000 fans crowded into the Arena for the hockey games, and an additional 500,000 persons patronized the other events staged in the facility in that first year. (A rodeo alone drew 98,000 customers.)

Sutphin's genius didn't end with the changes he wrought in the physical structure and the hockey team. He knew hockey fans were made, not born, and that familiarity bred future fans. Looking towards future generations of customers, he organized a scholastic hockey league whose teams would compete in the Arena in off-hours. He personally donated complete equipment for 12 high school teams and persuaded Barons players to serve as coaches of the schoolboy squads. In addition, Sutphin imported six talented hockey players from Minneapolis to provide a nucleus for an amateur hockey league—one, incidentally, that went on to set attendance records.

The owners of arenas in other cities looked on in admiration as the Sutphin whirlwind cut a swathe through professional sports circles and trailblazed a path for hockey. What was happening in Cleveland was a reversal of the usual order of things. Such innovations normally would be expected as a result of major league policy. Instead, a minor league owner was setting the pace and showing the way.

It was generally conceded that Cleveland would soon acquire one of the existing franchises in the NHL. Montreal had two at the time, the Maroons and the Canadiens, neither of which was prospering financially. It was assumed that one of those two teams —probably the Maroons— would end up in Cleveland.

That scenario probably would have been played out just as the script read had Al Sutphin given his assent. The fans in Cleveland were clamoring for an NHL franchise. The city was major league in every other sport and ready to step up to the same level in hockey.

Like most fans, Sutphin craved the prestige of the NHL, but the Champ had reason to hold back. There were practical considerations that could not be ignored. The Barons, a team with a minor league payroll, were outdrawing some of the NHL teams that were burdened with big league expenses. Would it be wise to exchange the success and profit of the Barons for a borderline future in the NHL? He had a heavy mortgage to pay off and had invested to the limit in his reconstituted team.

More important, Sutphin could not abandon his fellow AHL owners. They were his friends, his competitors, and, in a sense, his partners. Without Sutphin and the Cleveland franchise, the American League would be in serious jeopardy. The Barons played to overflow crowds wherever they went. Many of the smaller market teams in the league were struggling.

What to do?

In the end, Sutphin chose to enjoy the prosperity of the moment and bide his time on any promotion into the NHL. While the NHL owners were unhappy with Al's decision, Sutphin's AHL counterparts were forever thankful for his loyalty.

Meanwhile, Bill Cook's Barons were making Sutphin look very good with sure-handed play on ice. They were well on their way to dominating the league as they won the western division title in their first year under Cook. It was the kind of scenario that should have had all Clevelanders rooters shaking the rafters with their cheers, and most fans were doing just that.

But it's hard to please everyone, especially a sportswriter whose specialty is looking at the dark side of life. *Cleveland Press* columnist Carl Shatto was troubled by the abundance of victories in the Barons win column.

"Cleveland hockey fandom will awaken one of these mornings with an extremely painful attack of indigestion," Shatto warned. "Success is sweet, to be sure, but the cake of victory, like any other dessert, loses its flavor when downed too frequently....

"Their Barons today are leading the league...undefeated at the Arena, where they have piled 12 conquests on top of three ties. Night after night these new fans come out to see their favorites win, and they do...

"Home defeats, had they come earlier, probably would have incurred only slight displeasure. But not now. Victory now is taken as a matter of course, and in it there can be no element of surprise.

"Sutphin is supposed to be building for eventual Cleveland entry into the National League. He may be building so well as to defeat his own purpose. A newly-assembled National League team would have trouble winning even half its home games. And what a shock this would be to those new fans!"

Shatto's strange essay may have been the first time in journalistic history that a sports columnist publicly complained about the excellence of the home team and called on the management and players to lose a game once in a while. But the Barons refused to heed his advice.

Shatto would have been glad to learn that real problems were brewing with the Barons. When a team is winning, everything looks smooth to the fans, but sometimes victory conceals inner turmoil, masked by success on the ice. The Barons had their troubles from time to time, even as they dominated the league, and Sutphin knew enough about the game and the players to detect the latent unrest. What it came down to was that some of the players didn't like the coach.

Bill Cook was a hard taskmaster who demanded full-out effort and the best of each individual on the team. Some players thought the coach set too fast a pace and demanded too much.

The situation came to a head when two Barons stars, Lorne Duguid and Bob Griese, asked for a conference with Sutphin and told him that a revolt was brewing on the squad and that they, individually, had decided

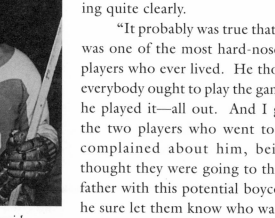

Lorne Duguid

not to play for Bill Cook any longer.

Jim Sutphin remembers the uprising quite clearly.

"It probably was true that Bill Cook was one of the most hard-nosed hockey players who ever lived. He thought that everybody ought to play the game the way he played it—all out. And I guess that the two players who went to Dad and complained about him, being stars, thought they were going to threaten my father with this potential boycott. Well, he sure let them know who was boss.

"That same night he called John Harris of the Pittsburgh Hornets and said, 'John, I'd like to send you Bob Griese.'

"Harris couldn't figure that out. He wanted to know if Griese had a bad leg or what.

"Dad said, 'No, there's nothing wrong with him, It's just that I don't like his face anymore.'

"He then called Lou Jacobs in Buffalo and said, 'Lou, I want to send Lorne Duguid to you.'"

When the rebellious players took their dressing rooms that same night, there was a sign on the bulletin board that announced the sale of Duguid and Griese to Buffalo and Pittsburgh. The abrupt action by Al Sutphin shocked the team and, for that matter, the entire league. It ended the incipient mutiny before it started and established beyond question the authority not only of Sutphin, but also Bill Cook.

At the end of the season, Sutphin promoted Bill Cook to general manager of the Barons and hired Bun Cook as the new coach of the team. It was an action that plainly represented another vote of confidence in the Cook family.

While Sutphin gave the Cooks and other Barons officials free rein in their management duties, he was deeply involved in the team's fortunes. He knew the game and he was a good judge of talent. He even worked out a system of merits and demerits by which he graded players.

As owner of the Barons, he took an active role in the makeup of the team. He was always willing to make a trade if he thought it would help, and most of his swaps turned out well.

"One of the most difficult trades my father ever made was when he traded Tommy Burlington," Jim Sutphin recalls.

Bill Cook, Al Sutphin & Fred "Bun" Cook

"Burlington was probably the greatest stick handler who ever played in the American League. He literally could take the puck from one end of the rink to the other and put it in the net, faking the goalie out of position. He didn't have too many assists. He wasn't really a good team player.

"Anyway, Dad had to make a decision in this case, and he decided to get a center who was more of a team player. This led him to make a trade that sent Burlington to Providence. It proved to be a highly unpopular move.

"On the other hand, one of his very best trades was pulled off in the 1947-48 season, when he traded Babe Pratt and Joe Cooper to the Hershey Bears for Hy Buller.

"Pratt and Cooper had had a tremendous playoff series in 1946-47 for Hershey, and Dad figured he just had to get those two guys. And he did. They were ex-National Leaguers who were at the trailing edge of their outstanding careers though, and they just didn't play well for the Barons, so Dad traded them back to Hershey for Buller. It was a great move.

"That was the year the Barons won 33 straight and went on to win the playoffs. They only lost one game in the playoffs!

"Dad was so sure the team was going to win the Calder Cup he had the championship rings made ahead of time. On the night the Barons won the last game of the finals in 1948, he was able to present the rings to the players in the dressing room! That's how much confidence he had in that team.

The hockey fans who jammed the Arena through those successful Al Sutphin-Bill Cook years had to be among the happiest anywhere. Despite what Carl Shatto wrote about the painful aspects of victory, the fans never seemed to tire of watching the Barons win.

Hy Buller

Needless to say, Sutphin himself inhaled the sweet smell of team success more deeply than anyone else because the winning ways of the Barons also were responsible for the steady reduction in the Arena's mortgage. It also meant that the lure of the National Hockey League faded as the years passed.

The Barons won the western division championship of the league in the 1937-38 season, won the American Hockey League Championship and the coveted Calder Cup in 1938-39, claimed division honors again in 1941, 1944, and 1945, and went on to the AHL crown in '41 and '45. Appropriately enough, Sutphin's last title team was his finest. Years later, the *Cleveland Press* weighed the question, "Which was the greatest Cleveland hockey team of all?" and conceded that, while the 1963-64 squad was superb, the 1947-48 Barons were the all-time best.

"For the duration of their nine Calder Cup playoff games," the Press pointed out, "the 1963-64 Barons were invincible. They won the playoffs with nine straight victories. But for sheer power, class and achievement, most veteran observers regard the 1947-48 Barons as the greatest of all;

perhaps the greatest the league has ever seen. This was the team that had a fantastic record streak of 30 consecutive games without a defeat from late in January until the fourth game of the post-season playoffs."

The members of that remarkable squad included Johnny Bower, Bobby Carse, Hy Buller, Ab DeMarco, Bob Solinger, Roy Kelly and Fred Thurier.

CLEVELAND BARONS 1947-48
AMERICAN HOCKEY LEAGUE CHAMPIONS

On the morning of January 28, 1948, it was impossible to foresee that the Cleveland Barons of 1947-48 were to become the greatest team in the history of the American Hockey League.

That night they won and climbed out of fourth place in the league's Western Division. Despite continuing success, the club still trailed Pittsburgh by six full games as late as February 14.

But the steamroller had started. With Fred (Bun) Cook as coach, the Barons were moving — past Indianapolis, past Buffalo, past Providence and, on Febraury 28, past Pittsburgh.

The unprecedented drive continued until the undefeated streak — stood at 30 straight — a new professional record.

Two fine goalies, Johnny Bower and Roger Bessette, supported by a strong defense, held the enemy at bay.

But it was up front that the success story was written. Two of the AHL's finest forward combinations set the pace — Johnny Holota centering for Pete Leswick and Bobby Carse — Ab De Marco setting up plays for Roy Kelly and Bob Solinger, the rookie of the year. And, on the third line, cagey Fred Thurier was at his best.

A team with more than just power and finesse! A team with a heart! That was the Barons of 1947-48 — The American League's Greatest!

Front row, left to right: Augie Herchenratter, Fred Thurier, Church Russell, General Manager Norbert L. Stein, Roger Bessette, President Al Sutphin, Johnny Bower, Coach Fred "Bun" Cook, Ab DeMarco, Roy Kelly, Roger Gagne. Second row, left to right: Publicity Director Eddie Coen, Eddie Wares, Julian Sawchuk, Les Brennan, Gordon Davidson, Dan Sprout, Hy Buller, Tony Bukovich, George Allen. Third row, left to right: Chief Scout Gail Egan, Jack Lavoie, Pete Leswick, Bob Solinger, Johnny Holota, Bobby Carse, Lou Trudel, Trainer Walter Robertson.

Sutphin's Greatest Team, 1948 Barons

Carl Shatto was no longer a member of the sports staff of the *Cleveland Press* when those 1947-48 Barons were scorching the Arena ice. It was probably just as well. He would not have been able to withstand the pain of all those victories.

This much is certain. Nobody enjoyed that brilliant season more than Al Sutphin.

Overleaf: Starting Al's day on the right foot was a team effort ...!

In the SUTPHIN Home

CHAPTER NINE

ON THE HOME FRONT

During the three years of his life that he devoted to the Arena crusade, Al Sutphin literally lived apart, in his own world. Besides lengthy meetings with Arena investment prospects, he continued to take frequent sales trips in the interest of his ink company. It was double duty of the most demanding kind, and one of the side effects was that his presence within the family circle became a sometime thing.

There had to be times in the lonely hours when this self-propelled human dynamo found himself assailed by doubts about the course he had chosen, but he always turned an optimistic face toward the outside world, as well as the inside world—the one within his family walls.

The Champ loved that inner circle. As widely traveled as he was, and however powerful the draw exerted by the world of business and sports, he always kept a ring of protective wagons encircling his home precincts. This was his precious haven, a place that afforded him the utmost joy.

Every father keeps a fearful eye on his children as they grow up, knowing that the time is fast approaching when they will be tumbling out of the nest. Al Sutphin was no exception, but he did his best to delay the inevitable scattering of the brood.

One of his moves to ward off the inevitable was the edict that no one in the clan could attend a college away from Cleveland. He wanted them to live at home while gaining higher education.

A related rule was that none of the children could drive until senior year in high school. There was a lot of grumbling over that edict, but Al stood firm.

The deep sense of family evident in Al was a natural Sutphin trait, conspicuously apparent in his relationship with his own mother and father.

The family life of the Sutphins was made happier by the presence in their midst of the grandparents on both sides, Ernie and Elizabeth Sutphen and Florence Hoynes (Grandpa Michael Hoynes died in 1920, before his daughter's marriage).

"When any one of us were ill," recalled Mary, "both of our grandmothers would be on hand to lend some tender, loving care. I remember when I was only eight years old and recuperating from an attack of scarlet fever, Grandma Sutton taught me how to play solitaire."

The grandparents filled an important role in the Sutphin family history in quite another way at the outset of the Great Depression when the bank crash occurred. It was something else Mary remembered because it came about in the same year that she had scarlet fever.

"I remember my mother and father taking me with them when they went to Lynn Park for a 'summit' meeting with my grandparents. Dad had no cash. Later I learned his entire worth was in the Guardian Bank which had failed.

"Fortunately Grandpa Sutphen had some assets in Cleveland Trust which could be accessed, but it was Grandma Sutphen who really saved the day. It seems that one day, on her daily streetcar trip downtown, she had overheard a rumor that the banks were going to close, so she hotfooted it to her friendly neighborhood branch and withdrew her savings.

"Both families managed to live on this nest egg until other cash became available. She had $2,000 on deposit, which she somehow had stashed away out of her monthly household allowance, much to Grandpa Sutphen's amazement!"

Depression or no depression, the family got a lot of fun out of life. Inflation, deflation, stock markets and depression all are meaningless words in the lexicon of youth. A pair of words that did have meaning to the kids, and the adults, was Shore Acres. That was the name given to a cottage at the foot of E. 185th Street, north of Lake Shore Boulevard. A friend of the family, Warren Morris, president of Ostendorf Morris real estate firm, lived across the street from the Sutphins on Derbyshire Road, and it was he who offered use of the cottage to the family. The acceptance was immediate.

"Shore Acres," said Mary Elizabeth, "was a magical place for all of us. Mother and Dad did a lot of entertaining there, big dinner parties with lots of people.."

Mention of Shore Acres stirred Jane Sutphin Leitch's memory also.

"Dad knew how to grasp and hold an audience, " she said, "and his stage was Shore Acres every weekend in the early 1930s. He would invite three or four couples from among his ink customers as his guests. Perhaps 'victims' would be a better word.

"We kids were part of the plot he would hatch. Our jobs were to set the table, and that sounds innocent enough, but you have to understand that, when finished, the table had side dishes that exploded, silver

Al's greatest promotion ... the 1932 Olympians at Cleveland Stadium

ware that bent in two, water glasses that dripped on your dress or tie, and serving dishes that tipped sideways when manipulated from a control on mom's lap."

Young Mary Elizabeth also took advantage of the situation by selling soda pop at a nickel a drink and, even better, peddling what she called "bootleg beer" at 10 cents a glass.

"Dad had the beer cached in the garage," she explained.

No doubt Al Sutphin winced when he found out about Mary Elizabeth's bargain sale of his beer, but he also saw the humor of the situation.

"My innocent crime carried no punishment," she remembers.

Shore Acres was the scene of an especially important family celebration following the 1932 Olympic Games in Los Angeles. The Champ, who hardly ever missed a major athletic event, not only attended those games on the West Coast, he brought back with him to Cleveland a group from the track team representing Great Britain.

Some of the British track stars from that nation's world-wide empire were black, and while there was some family wonderment over the neighborhood reaction, the Sutphins housed the team and played the role of gracious hosts in a style which surprised nobody who knew them.

The foreign track stars were willing players in an Sutphin-sponsored special track meet in Cleveland, one in which he pitted these renowned Olympic stars against some hand-picked Cleveland athletes.

High-schooler Jesse Owens

Some experts thought the entire idea was preposterous, but they didn't know Al Sutphin. Nor did they appreciate the fact that among the runners that Al had booked for this improbable competition was an East Tech High School standout named Jesse Owens.

It would be another four years before Owens' incredible victories in the 1936 Olympic Games in Berlin would establish him as the greatest star in track and field history. But the preview of the talent in the Sutphin-sponsored meet in Cleveland was enough to turn the heads of experts everywhere because Owens the high school boy, beat some of the world's best.

In years to come, Al would describe this track meet in Cleveland as his greatest single sports promotion!

Baseball was the favorite sport in the Sutphin household before the family became preoccupied with hockey, and League Park, the old home of the Indians, was frequently the scene of Sunday outings for the family. They would sit in the General Manager's box, courtesy of Al's friend Bill Evans.

Sutphin could never sit still at a baseball game any more that he could at a hockey match. There simply were too many friends in the stands, on the field, and in the press box, and he felt compelled to dart all over the ball park with handshakes and hellos. Grandma Hoynes, wise to this fact of life, was the one who stayed with the children in the Evans box to serve as baseball commentator and family disciplinarian.

The family anthology bulges with baseball stories, each reflecting a facet of the Sutphin personality.

"He definitely liked to have fun, and sometimes he would give us an assignment that we thought to be pretty bizarre," said Jim Sutphin, "but nobody ever had the nerve to argue the point. One time he arranged a softball game between the Braden-Sutphin Inky Pirates and the grandchildren at Woodhill Park. A few days before the game, he called me and said he wanted to have a bugler on hand to salute the players coming onto the field.

"A bugler?" I said.

"That's right," he said. "A bugler."

It was the end of our conversation as far as he was concerned. I turned to Norbert Stein at the other desk in our Arena office.

"Well," he said, "what's your problem? Your father wants a bugler. Get him a bugler."

"You could never say no to Dad. I called Dick Kroesen who knew everybody in town and said, 'Uncle Dick, I've got to have a bugler.'

"Well,' said Dick, not at all surprised, 'I know the guy at Randall Park Race Track—you know, the guy who wears the spats and the red cap—who blows the horn at the start of the day's races. Maybe I can get him to go out to Woodhill.'

"Sure enough, the guy in the fancy outfit showed up at Woodhill in time for the game. He was there only about 30 seconds. When the team ran out on the field, he blew his bugle as loud as could be. We gave him fifty bucks, he got in his car and drove away.

"You don't forget stuff like that."

Jane Leitch's earliest recollection of her father was of Sunday morning games of 'Rough and Tumble.'

"We were four little girls, ages 5 to 1, and we went wild when Daddy got down on all fours and played growling bear—we all attacked him, rolling him over and climbing all over him until he finally fell asleep on his back. That was just what we had been waiting for! We couldn't mess up his hair fast enough. We didn't know another Dad with a center part, so we always rushed to part his hair on the side, knowing that when he woke up, he would come to his feet, find a mirror, and come roaring after us while we scattered, yelling and laughing."

When Eddie Cantor sang, the Sutphins listened

Sunday evening proved to be a special family time also.

"We had sandwiches and soup, picnic style, in the living room every Sunday evening. We sat in the dark with only a hearth fire for light, awaiting the Chase & Sanborn theme song on the radio and the announcement of the *Eddie Cantor Hour*. No conversation allowed—if you spoke, you were sent to bed. We loved that hour together, and we loved Eddie Cantor."

"Dad loved show business and performers. Ethel Merman was his all-time favorite singer. We went to opening night at the Hanna for years and years, and, of course, the Arena gave Dad a chance to book his own shows and performers.

"Sometimes a star would stay with us or come out for dinner. Hazel Franklin of the Ice Follies and her mother once stayed with us for a week while appearing in Stars on Ice. Hazel was billed as the youngest skating star in the world, having been a star in England at age 12. She was so tiny she was only the size of my 11-year-old sister, but she actually was my age, 15."

Another dinner guest at the Sutphin table from the world of show business was one known simply as The Baron.

"The Baron was a 3-foot tall midget who came to dinner when my baby brother, Cal, was 2 years old," recalled Jane. "Cal was wearing a blue romper suit with big pearl buttons. The Baron was wearing a full dress suit, white tie and tails. They were exactly the same size and height! I will never forget the look on Cal's face when the Baron shook his hand and spoke to him in a man's voice!"

Mother Mary was not the type to seek the limelight. She did tolerate it as a part of her husband's life, like arctic air conditioning and heavy cigar smoke, but she never had any urge to compete with the Champ for the starring role beyond the family stage. Her solid scale of values told her that home itself was the most rewarding theater, and her children were the most interesting players in life's continuing drama, just as her religion provided the best possible script for daily living.

"Mom was just as solid as a rock. Truly a saint," said Jim Sutphin. "We affectionately called her 'Pamphlet' Mary. It seemed like every time we got a letter from her, there was a new prayer in the envelope.

There never was any clash between the principal forces in Mary Sutphin's book, but there was a time when, thanks to a comic combination of circumstances, Mary found herself blushing and laughing at the same time.

On the day that Mary Sutphin was to remember so well, her husband asked to keep young Jimmy home from school to accompany him to suburban Hudson where he was scheduled to meet the legendary cowboy star, Gene Autry, coming to Cleveland to star in a rodeo at the Arena.

"Jimmy and I will board Autry's train and ride in to the Cleveland Union Terminal with him," Al told his wife. "It should be a big thrill for him to meet a famous cowboy."

Mary acknowledged that distinct probability and gave her consent. The meeting in Hudson went as scheduled. Young Jimmy not only got to meet Gene Autry, he even had his picture taken sitting on Autry's knee by a *Cleveland Press* photographer. It was a thrill beyond description.

Al returned his young son to Mary that noon, and she gave him a note to give to his teacher when he returned to classes class after lunch. The note said simply that Jimmy had not been feeling well that morning, and would the teacher please excuse his half-day absence.

Jimmy took the note to school and handed it to his teacher. About that time, one of the little girls in the class came back from lunch bearing

Gene Autry & young Jimmy

a copy of the *Cleveland Press* for everyone to see. There, at the top of the front page, was a picture of Gene Autry holding Jimmy Sutphin on his lap!

"It was probably the only time in my mother's whole life that she told a lie," said Jim. "When she learned about the newspaper photo and realized that she had been caught, she was mortified."

One of the many things that set the Sutphin household apart from that of the average family was the coming and going of the head of the family himself. The Champ's wanderlust never relinquished its hold on him. In his busiest years, he somehow found the time to make one of his European trips. His young offspring took those pilgrimages in stride, assuming that all daddies were globetrotters.

Jane Leitch remembers the return of her father from one of those trips.

"After World War I, Dad traveled back to France, totally smitten with the French countryside and the friendship of a young fellow named Pierre Guilot and his family in Pierrefitte.

"While he was gone, we worried a lot about him crossing a huge ocean. This is 1929 and Carolyn was three.

The hectic pace was non-stop for Al, his family knew only too well

"As Dad ran up the driveway upon his return, Mother was standing in the doorway with Carolyn in her arms.

"Dad rushed up to Carolyn and said, 'Where's your Daddy?'

"And Carolyn said, 'On a big boat!'"

Al got the message, and swore he would spend more time on the home front, but the dilemma continued to plague him. His business and sports activities continued to multiply, along with his family, until it seemed as if a paltry 24 hours in a day weren't half enough. It would be almost 20 years before he finally took the drastic steps necessary to cure the problem.

Jim, Al & Cal at home on Berkshire Road, 1948

The Sutphin Children
l. to r., Carolyn, Mary E., Cal, Jane, Alberta & Jim

l. to r., Mr. & Mrs O.M. Garber
(Garber Printing Co.), Al &
Mary & unidentified couple

left, Florence Hoynes
Mary's mother
Michael's wife

Al expounds on the evils of "bad lies" to his very attentive sons, Jim & Cal

Overleaf: ... just another day for "Champ"

CHAPTER TEN

A SPORTS INCUBATOR

One of the imperatives that could not be ignored in the operation of the Arena was the need to find attractions that would keep the new facility busy year round. Professional hockey was the bread-and-butter event, but the menu needed to be expanded if the public appetite for entertainment were to be satisfied on a profitable basis.

This was a fact of life recognized by all of the arena owners in the larger American cities, and when Sutphin joined the group he was enthusiastically received by his peers. They knew just enough about him to recognize that he was a highly enterprising newcomer who was bubbling over with original ideas that would benefit one and all.

If those Sutphin talents needed spurring at any time in his career, it was when the Arena opened its doors to the public in 1937. The fear of financial failure was the spur that drove the Champ on to his greatest heights then, because if the Arena were not solidly booked, the ever-present specter of bankruptcy shimmered as a future possibility.

Some of the attractions that he was able to book into the Arena were already fan favorites. The 6-day bicycle races, for example, had become well-known to Clevelanders when they were staged at Cleveland Public Hall, and stars like Torchy Peden and Reggie McNamara had become favorites in this unlikely sport which called for continuous, around-the-clock competition. Dedicated fans swarmed the Arena, literally at all hours, to watch the inexhaustible bikers speed by while sensible people were asleep in their beds.

The bike races were but one attraction that made the switch from Public Hall to the Arena. The annual K. of C. Track Meet was another important addition to the Arena calendar, as were many of the big-name boxing and wrestling matches.

A fortunate coincidence at the time the Arena was coming into being was the emergence on the entertainment scene of a show called the *Ice Follies*. The creation of two brothers, Roy and Ed Shipstad and their partner, Oscar Johnson, this was an elaborate musical show on ice. Its inspiration undoubtedly was to be found in the popular motion pictures that starred Sonja Henie, Swedish ice skating champion. The com-

Sonja Henje congratulates Arena bike marathon winners, Al looks on

bination of such skating skill on ice with all the imaginative theatrics of show business proved to be irresistible when the *Ice Follies* came into being in 1936.

When the popular ice show shared honors with the hockey teams on the opening week program of the Arena, the Shipstads and Al Sutphin hit it off well together. The *Ice Follies* of 1938, with Roy Shipstad and Bess Erhardt, was booked for a five-night run beginning on the night of November 10th. The show was an unqualified hit in Cleveland; a novelty phase of show business that the customers greeted with high enthusiasm and gratifying presence at the box office.

Windsor French of the *Cleveland Press* was completely captivated by the performance of the *Ice Follies* on that historic opening night.

"That anyone can stand on a pair of skates at all is miracle enough for me," he wrote. "But when it is combined with incarnate grace, my heart simply ceases to function. Nothing so cool, fresh and entirely beautiful ... can ever become boring. In the unhappy event that it should, the management has provided a comfortable and well stocked bar."

The only trouble with the *Ice Follies* was that it was one of a kind.

The Ice Capades (1960)

It could be booked only once a year because it was in heavy demand in arenas all over the country. The public appetite for that new form of entertainment obviously called for more, and because of that apparent demand, it was Sutphin who led the way in the organization of another traveling ice show—the *Ice Capades.*

Among those who joined with Sutphin in this enterprise was the well-known theatrical magnate, John Harris of Pittsburgh. He, the owner of the Duquesne Gardens in that city, became the show's president and producer. When the *Ice Capades* debuted in 1940, it was an immediate hit.

The existence of two ice shows worked out nicely for all the ice rink operators around the nation. One would play the Cleveland Arena in the autumn-winter season and the other would be featured in the spring-summer season. The audience approval rating was so high that each of the shows easily won capacity audiences.

The Champ looked upon the *Ice Capades* with more than a little pride whenever it played in the Arena. Not only had he been a leading force in the creation of the show, and one of its owners, he actually had encountered resistance to its creation from some of his own Arena directors—a fact he chose not to reveal until some 20 years later in a letter to some old friends.

What prompted the letter was a congratulatory editorial in the *Cleveland Press* in October, 1959:

Ice Capades Has Grown Up
to Million-Dollar Venture

"It was almost 20 years ago—Feb. 14, 1940—that Al Sutphin, former Arena impresario, met with six other Arena managers at the Hershey Hotel and organized the Ice Capades. Each man chipped in $5,000 and the original budget of the enterprise was set at $27,000.

"On Feb. 26, 1941, Sutphin brought the Ice Capades to the Arena for the first time. Here as everywhere else that the glamorous, exciting show performed, the new kind of entertainment caught on. Now Ice Capades is back at the Arena, presenting its 20th edition. To give you an idea how it has grown, this current edition was bankrolled at $100,000.00.

"The ice show has in it something to appeal to everyone—beauty of costumes, pageantry, youth, speed, thrills, comedy. No wonder it has established itself as such a great success."

Al Sutphin's follow-up letter explained its origins:

"Dear Gang:

"Personally I have never been a gambler in stocks and bonds. My three ventures were in Braden-Sutphin, Cleveland Arena, and Ice Capades.

"And that's the total!

"Oh yes! And the Braden-Sutphin Farms.

The writer put $12,000 in Ice Capades back in 1939, and this stock has paid $12,000 per year ever since, amounting to 100% per year.

"However, I bought this stock personally, inasmuch as Carl Lezius and other directors of the Cleveland Arena did not believe in this show. In fact, I would not even book it into our own building. I therefore rented the Cleveland Arena and had two marvelous successful years booking the show myself.

"Knowing that it would not look right to the rank and file stockholders, I sold the stock and transferred the show to the Arena, although

I could have explained to the stockholders easily enough that I had a very timid Board of Directors who had turned the venture down!"

The Ice Follies were a great attraction and the Ice Capades a spectacular innovation, both perennial successes at the House That Al Built, but neither was the all-time box office champion. That honor went to a

Sonya Henie

solo act, the diminutive Queen of the Ice who also proved to be Sutphin's most challenging conquest.

Sonja Henie was an Olympic winner at fifteen, a touring pro at eighteen and a movie idol by twenty, so taken was the worldwide public with the fair-haired Swedish maiden's beauty and grace on the ice.

By the late 1930's, she was still at the peak of her career, a veteran of more than a dozen world tours. She commanded a hefty fee for her one-night shows in the grandest showplaces of the major cities of every continent. Al Sutphin wanted her for the Arena.

When cables and telegrams to her manager brought only a luke-warm response, Al turned on the charm. He learned that Sonja was not only the star of her own show, she was also the brains behind it, making the business decisions as well as the artistic ones. Al vowed to ingratiate himself enough to gain access to her inner circle and ultimately negotiate a deal with the little lady, man-to-woman. It wasn't going to be easy.

Al & Sonja

Having memorized the itinerary for her upcoming U. S. tour, Al pursued her: first to New York, where she wouldn't see him before the show because she was too busy; then to Philadelphia, where she wouldn't see him after the show because she was too tired. Finally, in Buffalo, he was granted a brief audience. Sutphin managed to convince Miss Henie to at least visit his Arena in Cleveland to see for herself if it wasn't an ideal forum for her peerless act.

After a VIP tour, with Al conjuring up visions of a packed Arena greeting her with a thunderous standing ovation, Sonja was noncommittal.

"It's nice," she said.

Eventually, they got down to business. She liked Sutphin, admired his Arena, and told Al she would accept an offer, but she wouldn't accept his terms.

"If you want Sonja, you have to pay for Sonya, Mr. Zutphin."

Al reminded her that the facility itself was so beautiful, people were willing to pay 25 cents to see it on tours.

"Good", she said, "for the building they pay twenty-five cents, then for Sonja and the building they pay $2.50!"

She had him, and she wouldn't budge. For one of the few times in his entire career, Al capitulated in a deal. Although she never failed to

Arena Night Life (1949)

attract less than a sellout crowd whenever she performed at the Arena in the years that followed, Sutphin would later remember her more for the money than the show. When asked in the 1960's for his comment on the escalating costs of sports stars, the Champ just smiled and shook his head.

"Son", he said, "I could have had a whole team of hockey players or basketball players for what I paid Sonja Henie for two nights a year."

The Arena proved to be an invigorating force in the community, an exciting new venue with an endless series of thrilling attractions. At the same time, downtown generally had gone into a skidding spiral as the depression worsened. Theater and restaurant revenues had declined markedly and many of the luxurious movie theaters had taken on the drab look of neglect. Among the many glittering jewels on Playhouse Square, only the Hanna Theater still featured stage plays and kept its marquee lighted through the dreary years.

Suddenly there was the Arena, instilling new life to that stretch of Euclid Avenue once called Millionaires' Row. Until Sutphin, that area's future seemed destined to be linked with used car lots and derelict mansions, fated to stand empty as decrepit testimony to lost glory.

The Arena not only offered a smorgasbord of sports and theatrics, it was a draw in itself.

"Going to the Arena was like going to the Hanna Theater," recalled Jim Sutphin. "Believe it or not, people got dressed up to go to

The S. S. Inx

the hockey game. Camel hair coats and even ties, you know. The Arena then was the place to go, and it usually was sold out. The admission tickets in 1949 were very, very reasonable. The top-priced ticket was only $2.40!"

The Sutphin family shared in the fun. Grandmother Sutphen, the lady known as Sutton, and her husband, Grandfather Ernie Sutphen, had season tickets to the Arena and went to all the games, sometimes taking the children with them.

"And then," said Jim Sutphin, "there was the place we called the ship. It was something special."

The "ship" really was special. Far from being seaworthy, it was a landlocked part of the Braden-Sutphin Ink Company Building to the north of the Arena and bore an appropriate name, *the S. S. Inx.*

What Sutphin created in the large room of nautical design was a place which could be used for the entertainment of customers, friends, press and radio. It tied the ink company to the sports arena, and it won instant popularity as a colorful place to gather after a hockey game or feature show on any given night. The room looked like the stern end of a ship and Al had tried mightily to create a realistic setting.

A writer for the *St. Louis Globe-Democrat* called it "the Yacht that Never Moves" in a special feature article for his newspaper. From the tone and length of the piece, it seemed that he was more impressed by *the S.S. Inx* than the splendid new Arena he had traveled to Cleveland to write about.

"Al Sutphin has a yacht on which he entertains 12 months out of every year," he wrote. "And to date no one has complained of frostbite, even when frigid winds whip across Lake Erie; and the only proximity of ice on Al's yacht is the cube you've got in your highball glass."

The writer conceded that "a yacht in an ink factory is a rather odd circumstance, but is highly practical for Al Sutphin, a semi-alert, semi-stout, non-modest type of executive whose awareness of the value of salesmanship has put him into the upper income tax brackets."

"The idea for the built-in ship, he explained, came to Sutphin when he was putting together his Arena and ink company complex of buildings.

"With an eye on sales promotion through entertaining, he incorporated into the plant plans his idea for the yacht...his entertaining bailiwick embraces the aft deck of a yacht, complete with sails, lifeboat stations where lifeboats hang on davits, a simulated hand-pegged maple floor, a ship's bell, a door for non-existent crew quarters, passageways, portholes, the aforementioned anchor—and a bar.

"Surrounding both exposed sides of the yacht, and also at its rear, is painted scenery—on canvas that moves up and down. The scenery is a typical lake view on all sides, including ships in the distance, a lighthouse, cliffs and seagulls. The illusion, as the scenery moves is, of course, that the S.S. Inx is rocking, and the more one watches these ersatz horizons go rhythmically up and down, the more convinced one becomes that the blooming thing is actually tempting *mal de mer*.

"To carry the illusion to even more realistic heights, Al has installed a sieve device containing marbles and navy beans, and this gadget operates in unison with the canvas drops. The effect is a definite swish, not too loud, yet not too soft. Thus, both through optic and aural shenanigans, is the gag carried to its fullest."

Sutphin recalled, for the reporter's benefit, a story about a woman guest who fell victim to his dry land theatrics. After she had been on board the *S. S. Inx* only a few minutes, with the backdrop heaving and the sea-going sound effects, the poor woman began to clutch the railing.

"Sutphin had to escort her to a comparatively uninteresting area," the visiting writer noted, no doubt anxious himself to get back to St. Louis to tell his newspaper buddies about the strange stuff going on in Cleveland. In an ink factory, of all places!

The "Ship" got one of its heaviest workouts in 1954, an outstanding year for Cleveland baseball fans, of whom Al Sutphin was among the most rabid. Not only did the Indians win the American League pennant that year, the city also was the scene of the annual All Star Game.

1954 All Star game
l. to r., Al Rosen, Ted Williams, Mickey Vernon & Mickey Mantle

In his usual big hearted way, Sutphin invited 300 guests to the big game. He treated them all to a party behind the outfield fence in Cleveland Stadium prior to the game, seizing the opportunity for one of his outrageous gags. Each guest was given a box of popcorn with a special message inside the box on an index card, and each card was attached by sewing-type thread to each and every popcorn kernel in the box. When the card was pulled out, the entire box of popcorn spilled out.

The post-game party was held on the deck of Al's *S.S. Inx* out on Chester Avenue. Never was the ship's seaworthiness tested as fully as it was on that memorable day.

Unfortunately, when Braden-Sutphin Ink Company moved to East 93rd Street in 1957, the "ship" remained behind. It was missed terribly by one and all as it disappeared over the horizon with all the other creations of the ship's master.

Al never quit selling...this time with the Cleveland Skating Club

105 •

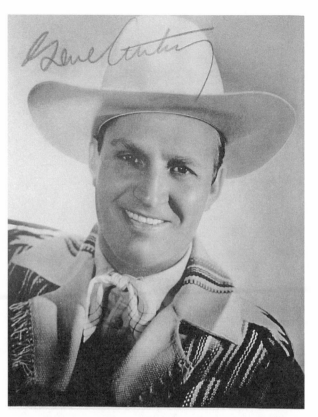

Bob Hope plays the Arena

Gene Autry was always a main attraction

The Winter Thrill Circus made a regular appearance at Al's "Ice House" on Euclid Ave.

The Arena Menu, circa 1945

Al & Mary skating through life together

"Al conjured up every event imaginable to sell out his "Million Dollar Gamble on Euclid Avenue"

*Al , Mary, Jane & Friends with Roy Rogers,
Arena Attraction*

*Another night of "Ice Magic" at the
Arena... early 1940's*

Overleaf: The Sutphin Band plays a tune...1920

The Sutphin band are playing a tune of Merry Christmas and Good Wishes for the New Year for you

N'est-ce pas

MERRY CHRISTMAS TO ALL

ON Christmas Day, 1918, greetings were mailed to my friends from this "Old Shack" at Pierrefitte-sur-Meuse, France, in the historic "St. Mihiel Salient", and now comes "The Season's Best" from

THE BRADEN PRINTING INK CO.

Al Sutphin

Christmas Day, 1918, the first of a long tradition

MERRY CHRISTMAS TO ALL
OVER THE YEARS

THE SUTPHIN FAMILY CHRISTMAS CARD

As with so many other endeavors in Al Sutphin's career, the initial Braden Sutphin Christmas card was an impulsive master stroke designed to bring a little good cheer to everyone Al knew. Now, seventy-five years later, the time honored tradition continues as holiday greetings circulate among more than 5000 friends, relatives and customers across the United States and in over a dozen foreign countries.

The Christmas card originated in 1918. Al Sutphin, along with boyhood friends, Al Betz, Bill Reiser, Dan Hoynes and Dwight Walker, were waiting to be mustered out after the armistice of 1918, ending World War I. Ever the salesman, Al seized on the unique opportunity to combine patriotism and promotion in a holiday greeting to customers back home.

That first card was a black-and-white, 3-1/2 inch square photo-drawing depicting the historic St. Mihiel Solient district, postmarked from Pierrefitte, France.

It began a Christmas tradition as constant as Santa Claus.

OVER THE YEARS…

I rule the House of Sutphin, I do

I wish You A Merry Christmas And a very Happy New Year, I do

Mary and Al Sutphin sincerely wish you all of that, too

Four years later, Al Sutphin married Mary Hoynes and the 1922 card reflected that event. Another historic custom had begun. From then on, Christmas Card recipients would be regaled with the milestones, highlights and accomplishments of three generations of the Sutphin family, with new members arriving as regularly as the card itself.

By 1923, Mary Elizabeth had arrived and that year's card quotes her as saying "I rule the House of Sutphin, I do!" The same words were used on future cards for subsequent arrivals Jim and Cal, and again when Al fell in love with his disobedient dog, "Fanta", (a love all six children considered misplaced).

For the first time, the 1925 card included a calendar, a welcome staple for years, finally replaced by the ever-popular "story" cards. Competing only with himself, Sutphin felt obliged to make the stories bigger and better every year. It wasn't long before the annual greeting rivaled a Hollywood production in scope and characters.

1925

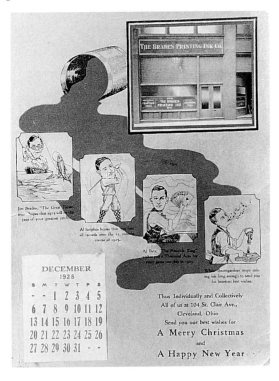

1930

The 1930 card showed Al Sutphin in an airplane dropping ink on England and France, generating wide circulation in those countries ever since. Once Al Sutphin sold you ink, you were his friend forever, and like it or not, you became a permanent name on the mailing list.

The Christmas Card announced the births of all six Sutphin children. Through the years it showed them in groups, always with a Champ-inspired theme: once in church pretending to be pious; another time tearing the house apart. One of the more memorable cards featured the Sutphin children and wife Mary, caricatured as Falcon hockey players.

1936

1947

More than once, the Story behind the Card became a Sutphin classic. Once, in the mid 1940's, Al was returning from a long and successful sales trip and stopped in a downtown establishment to celebrate his good fortune. By chance, he met an out-of-town salesman, a young man on his first trip through his new territory in Northeast Ohio. The two outgoing peddlers struck up an immediate friendship and the merriment carried on throughout the night, and then the following day, and again the next. By the end of the week however, Sutphin's new companion was both worried and despondent. He had trailed the gregarious Champ through every night spot and gathering point in Cleveland, failing to make even one sales call. He would certainly lose his new job and his family would be the worst for it.

"What do you sell?", asked Sutphin.

"Bibles", the man explained.

A huge smile crossed over the Champ's countenance.

"What would be a good-sized order in your territory?"

"Well, probably 400 or 500 bibles in a week," answered the man.

Al told him to be sure to stop by Braden Sutphin later that day. When he appeared at Sutphin's office that afternoon, the Champ handed the salesman a purchase order for 5,000 bibles marked 'price advise.' In utter disbelief, the salesman asked what Al would do with 5,000 bibles. Then Sutphin explained that he had been searching for a unique idea for his annual Christmas card. Now he had it.

That year's card was to feature Al and Mary sitting in front of their fireplace reading the bible with every card accompanied by a copy of the Good Book. Mary Sutphin stepped in at that point and put her foot down. As a good, practicing Irish Catholic, she was not going to be photographed reading the Gideon(i.e., Protestant)Bible. So it was that the Christmas card instead featured Al and Mary drinking tea in front of the fireplace. Al did, however, distribute the 5,000 bibles and a salesman somewhere in Indiana was thanking God for a miracle comparable to the loaves and fishes.

1954

    The Champ had decided a cowboy theme was in order for the 1954 card. At Ft. Meyers, Ray and Alberta Stoney were notified to line up a donkey, two wicker baskets, cowboy gear and a photographer.

    The oldest child in each of the families was to be astride the donkey while the younger ones were placed in the baskets. Well, the winds blew, cowboy hats flew, baskets tipped, children flipped, donkeys bolted, and the photographer revolted.

    And the Card? It showed children in baskets, frowns all around, and no cowboy hats on either Matt or Ray Stoney. The Champ was neither happy nor impressed!

Several cards commemorated Al and Mary's trips to Europe and around the world, family reunions, anniversaries and special events. The Arena, the Barons and the Ice Capades emerged in feature roles. Guest stars appeared in abundance. The 1957 card alone included sports greats Lou Groza, Paul Brown, Danny Murtaugh, Jimmy Dykes, Herb Score and Joe Gordon coaching benches full of Sutphin grandchildren.

1961

    1961 may have set the record for production complications. The plan was to photograph all the youngsters on a serene Lake Erie outing, dressed in their Sunday best aboard the Sutphin boat. Unfortunately, two of the children fell into the lake; four others were so seasick they had to be propped up for the picture; and Margaret Leitch, at eighteen months, shrieked when she saw the rough water and refused to go aboard. She finally appeared in a bait bucket on the front of the card with her great-grandfather, Ernie Sutphen, grandparents Al and Mary Sutphin, and her clever Aunt Mary, who had remained single. All sported sweet smiles.

If social commentary is important, Carolyn Leitch, Jr. can hold up the 1967 card for all to see. It featured the ten grandsons in the Board Room around the conference table and the eleven granddaughters at the typewriters. Such stereotyping did not discourage Carolyn, who became the first grandchild to take a seat on the Braden-Sutphin Board of Directors in 1993.

1960

Longtime family friend Betty Moran was the unsung and unseen hero of the 1960 card commemorating the 23rd anniversary of the Ice Follies. Spread across the Arena ice were eighteen grandchildren, all dressed in matching military-blue costumes with white crossed straps and brass buttons. Betty was pressed into service to sew the buttons on the costumes—211 on each for a total of 3,798 brass buttons! She never complained.

Ray Stoney, remembers the 1962 card only too well. The grandchildren were dressed in southern belle and beau costumes, out for a cruise on the "Braden-Sutphin Show Boat." Everything was going fine until Ray was forced to jump fully dressed into the Caloosachatchee River to keep the Show Boat from crashing into the dock. And he didn't complain either!

Jim and Louise Sutphin
Their children

Ray and Alberta Stoney
Their children ✝

Cal

C. E. "Dad" Sutphin

...phin Family wish you a *Merry Christmas*
and Ice-Capets for 1962 (First Edition)

✝   Matt ✝   Ray ✝   Robbie   Hal ★   Carolyn   Jim   Ann ✝   Dan

1962

A MERRY CHRISTMAS

FROM THE SUTPHINS

1982

The Sutphin Family Album
Season's Greetings

Adam Leitch 8/4/82

Amy Viecelli 7/12/75
Sara Viecelli 8/22/73

Brian Leitch 1/13/80

Megan Leitch 7/22/82

Justin Solack 12/13/81

Great-Grandmother Sutphin
and her Eleven Great Grandchildren

December 1982

Ray Stoney IV 9/1/82

Heather Fisher 9/2/72

Jennifer Leitch 7/21/78
Michael Leitch 7/28/80

Matt Viecelli 1/18/80

That may be the theme of the Sutphin Family Christmas Card.
No one ever complained—at least not when the Champ was within ear-
shot—and there are all those wonderful, lasting memories in living color.
Mostly red!

...A MERRY CHRISTMAS TO ALL!

Overleaf: The N.B.A., the Cleveland Caviliers vs. The Los Angeles Lakers, 1973

CHAPTER ELEVEN

THE BIRTH OF THE N.B.A.

A stellar attraction at the Arena from the very beginning was basketball, but only on the scholastic level. The professional brand of the game actually had a long history in Cleveland, but it was marked by highs and lows, as if the fans couldn't make up their minds about the game.

Ned Irish of Madison Square Garden was one of the pace-setters in the evolution of basketball as a major public attraction when he began booking collegiate double-headers. They filled the seats in Madison Square Garden, while single contests, even those featuring top college rivalries, had failed to draw. A ready explanation was that a single basketball game simply didn't last long enough and left the public grumbling that it had not gotten its money's worth.

A double-header headlining big-name college teams answered that complaint in New York and offered a lesson that was not ignored in other cities. Such basketball bills became common attractions nationally.

In Cleveland, the game was still in its introductory stage as a professional sport in the mid-30's. In fact, the city was something of a pioneer in the establishment of basketball as a box-office game, thanks to the efforts of a downtown retail merchant, Max Rosenblum, owner of a clothing store bearing his name on Euclid Avenue.

The very first sports event of note in the new Public Hall was a basketball game between the famous world champion Celtics and the Rosenblums. It was, by all accounts, an outstanding contest, won by the Celtics, 28 to 24. The early style of basketball obviously was defensive in nature. But what really was outstanding was that more than 10,000 Clevelanders paid to see it.

The 1920's also saw the formation of the first professional basketball league. Formally known as the American Basketball League, it had a Cleveland team entry sponsored by the same Max Rosenblum. That

team, managed by I. S. (Nig) Rose, won the league championship by beating the Brooklyn team in the 1926 finale.

The Rosenblums claimed the world basketball championship again with American League victories in 1929 and 1930 as the Celtics, unquestionably the greatest basketball team in the early years of the game, came under the sponsorship of the Clevelander and took on the name of the Rosenblum Celtics.

Its lineup of players included Joe Lapchick, Nat Holman, Carl Husta, Davey Banks, Dutch Dehnert: A *Who's Who* of the pioneer basketball days. The highly-regarded book, *24 Seconds to Shoot*, an informal history of the National Basketball As-

The "Original" Celtics

sociation by L. Koppett (MacMillan, N.Y., 1968) tells of Al Sutphin's role in the evolution of major league basketball and today's high-powered N.B.A.

"In the 1920s, when all commercial sports enjoyed a golden age, an American League, with teams in Cleveland, New York and Philadelphia had a brief period of major-league aura, but very brief. The respected teams were basically independents. First and foremost among them was the Original Celtics of New York. They played and won championships in various leagues, but made more money and reputation by touring and taking on local opponents.

"The game grew steadily on the high school and college level, but the pros were stagnating, primarily because there was no way to accommodate large crowds to generate consistent profits. More often than not, pro teams were sponsored by some business as a means of advertising that firm's name (e.g., the Cleveland Rosenblum-Celtics) ... At this point, other forces started to create large arenas ... but a "big expensive plant couldn't make money if it was not in use most of the year. Into this vacuum, a new sport moved. Ice hockey, imported from Canada, was an instant success. From every point of view, major league hockey was just the thing the new arena's were looking for."

But arenas couldn't survive on just that one sport, and, as Koppett pointed out, in 1946, at war's end, all the arena owners turned to the possibilities inherent in basketball.

The sport began enjoying popularity on the collegiate level, developing "an unprecedented glut of spectacular players on dozens of college teams," a talent supply that was augmented by athletes among the returning war veterans.

"In many minds, in many places, the thought was insistent...Why not put on, professionally, college style and college-atmosphere games with college developed players? And why not cash in on the economic advantages of an alliance between an arena and a promoter, the way (Ned) Irish and the Madison Square Garden did to their mutual benefit?"

Nig Rose

"These ideas were in the air, but in a few specific minds they were not just a thought; they were an intention.

"In Boston, a man named Walter Brown, and in Cleveland, a man named Al Sutphin, were about to join forces to bring into being what would eventually become today's National Basketball Association ..."

When the first organizational meeting to institute an arena-owned professional basketball league was held, Brown and Sutphin took the lead in rounding up support. It was they who brought in Maurice Podoloff, president of the American Hockey League, submitting his name for consideration as president of the new league, the Basketball Association of America. (Podoloff's family owned the New Haven Arena and AHL franchise).

The first meeting took place in New York on June 6, 1946. Charter members of the league, representing 11 teams altogether, included five franchise owners in the American Hockey League. Prominent among them was Al Sutphin of Cleveland, whose team was called the Cleveland Rebels. Boston, Chicago, Detroit, New York, Pittsburgh, Providence, St. Louis, Toronto and Washington were the other cities represented.

Manager of the Cleveland Rebels was Roy Clifford, who had been an outstanding coach at Western Reserve University. Coach of the Rebels was Dutch Dehnert, onetime star of the Celtics. Among the standout players on the team were Frankie Baumholtz, Mel Riebe and Ken Saylors.

Cleveland's first season of professional basketball at the Arena was clouded by the runaway skill of the Washington Capitols, under the leadership of Red Auerbach, then an unknown. They "ran off and hid from the rest," according to Koppett.

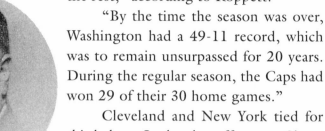

"By the time the season was over, Washington had a 49-11 record, which was to remain unsurpassed for 20 years. During the regular season, the Caps had won 29 of their 30 home games."

Cleveland and New York tied for third place. In the play-off games, Cleveland won the first contest, but New York claimed the remaining two.

Maurice Podoloff

"And so, on April 22, the first season of the B.A.A. had ended," noted Koppett. "In the sense that it had been completed at all, and that outstanding players had proved themselves, it could be called a success. But its impact on the public, in its own cities, was still quite secondary, and on the general sports public, nil. Financially there was a great deal of wreckage.

"The three trailing teams in the Western Division—Cleveland, Detroit, and Pittsburgh—closed up shop. They abandoned the original conception because they didn't have the resources, or the will, to keep spending money."

Al Sutphin's Rebels actually had a creditable record: 30 wins and 30 losses. A .500 percentage is not bad in any league; nor is third place.

What discouraged Sutphin was not the prospect of rising expenses, nor the failure of the team to win the title. What bothered him most was that two of Cleveland's leading sports editors, Whitey Lewis of the *Press* and Gordon Cobbledick of the *Plain Dealer*, took a dim view of professional basketball as a whole and spoke slightingly of the Cleveland Rebels and the new league—when they bothered to write about the sport at all. Sutphin had high regard for sports writers, and for Lewis and Cobbledick in particular. Their critical stance not only hurt the Rebels following among readers, but diminished Sutphin's own enthusiasm for the B.A.A. cause. He told friends and associates that if the two sports editors had taken a positive attitude toward the Rebels, he would not have hesitated to continue.

"Always sorry that we were forced to quit, Maurice. And I did not quit because of our losses," Sutphin declared in a letter to Podoloff in 1959.

"It just happened that two of our newspapers out of the three in Cleveland were most antagonistic to our so called 'race track' basketball.

In that same letter, Sutphin offered his thoughts on owner-ethics:

"Certainly too bad that owners in sports just have to win, and (that) players and angles are so important in their lives.

Al & the Cleveland Rebels

"Personally, I never saw a player who was worth the breaking up of friendship, and said so to every owner in our hockey league. Behind the door skullduggery used to make me sick....Guess there are always two ways of doing things..."

In the letter, Al acknowledged earlier correspondence from the N.B.A. president noting Sutphin's prominent mention in the 1958-59 guide book and history of the league:

"In the summer of 1946, as a result of the enterprise and energetic efforts of Mr. Walter A. Brown, President and Manager of the Boston Garden, and now owner of the Boston Celtics, and Mr. Al Sutphin, owner and operator of the Cleveland Arena, the owners and operators of the largest indoor arenas in the United States and Canada, men who had successfully promoted ice hockey, ice shows, rodeos and doubleheader college basketball, assembled to form a professional basketball league to present basketball on a major league basis to have similar status with major league professional sports — baseball, football and hockey."

Podoloff added: "I don't think that either you or Walter realized originally how important this professional basketball would be. One indication may be furnished by our television program, which started in 1953-54 with the telecasting of fourteen regular season games with a rights fee of $3,000 each....Our present agreement with NBC covers a total of twenty-five games...and the rights fee is $308,000.

Walter Brown, Celtics owner

"I know when you and Walter chose me to be the executive of the Association you wanted to do me a favor. I don't think you realized how great a one you did, and to both of you I have been everlastingly grateful."

As it was, the Cleveland Rebels never played a second season. But they did leave behind the glowing memory of one contest that remains unique in the annals of the B.B.A. and the N.B.A.

It was the first game of the Cleveland Rebels schedule, played against the New York Renaissance team in the Arena, which had been the scene of a Barons hockey game the previous night. A hardwood floor had been drawn over the ice to permit the basketball game to be played. Unfortunately, the floor had not been anchored properly, and, as the game proceeded, it began to literally come apart at the seams. So did the basketball game, as the moisture began to form on the wooden floor, causing the players to slip and slide all over the court. The contest began to take on the look of the hockey game played the previous night. All the players needed were skates.

Referee of the game was Hal Lebovitz, an outstanding player himself before moving on to distinction as a sports writer and editor for the *Cleveland News* and the *Plain Dealer*.

"There never was a basketball game like that Rebels opener," said Lebovitz who, like the players, slipped and slid all over the Arena floor in that real-life comedy routine.

Al Sutphin himself looked on in horror at the slippery-floor spectacle and at game's end he ordered all of the Arena's employees to stay on the job until the icy condition of the floor was corrected. It was sunrise before the crew that worked under Bill Wotsh, head of Arena maintenance, remedied the situation to the satisfaction of the angry Arena owner.

Whenever anybody brought up the subject of professional basketball, the B.A.A., the N.B.A., or the Cleveland Rebels to Al Sutphin in later years, he would only shake his head in sad recall. That aborted venture, and all the circumstances surrounding it, came together in his memory as the only major failure in any montage of his many dreams. This conclusion, however, grossly underestimated his own contribution and the major overall achievement, which was the creation of that institutional giant of the sports world, the National Basketball Association.

Hal Lebovitz

The Cleveland Rebels play at the Arena, 1946

Overleaf: Once There Was A Time And Place...

Once
There Was
A Time And Place.

CHAPTER TWELVE

DOWN ON THE FARM

The only important employee benefit that an ordinary worker enjoyed during the depression was the job itself. Very few companies provided any fringe benefits and it was the fortunate employee whose company provided paid vacation time.

In remarkable contrast to such conditions was a radical idea that evolved in the mind of Al Sutphin.

The Braden-Sutphin Ink Company was the Champ's first love on the business level and his affection for it never faltered, not even when the Arena and the Barons competed for his favor. He liked the ink business.

The men and women on the Braden-Sutphin payroll were almost as close to Sutphin's heart as blood relatives. Cynics have a way of dismissing paternalism as something almost evil today, but in the case of Sutphin, it was a nice mixture of generosity and genuine affection for the employees.

Perhaps the most extreme manifestation of the this sentiment was an idea that evolved into a jovial experiment in employer-employee relations.

What emerged from Al's imagination was the concept of a Florida resort that would serve as a place to entertain his family, his friends, and his business associates. But the idea went beyond that. As he saw it, such a place also would serve as a no-cost vacation site for his employees at Braden-Sutphin and the Arena and—this was the most surprising twist— ultimately it would become a kind of utopian retirement community for family and employees alike.

Choosing the Florida site for his private Shangri-La was not easy. He knew what he wanted and gave his blueprint to real estate agents and chambers of commerce representatives in a number of Florida areas.

The site had to be on the state's West Coast, on the Gulf of Mexico, and he and Mary searched relentlessly, much as Ponce de Leon had hunted for his fountain of youth centuries before. It was just as hard to find.

During a three-year period, the Sutphins chose each winter to concentrate their search in the area of De Leon Springs, near the city of

The Miles home

Deland, Florida, and it appeared that this would be the site of their choice until Al received a letter from his uncle, Will Clark, an executive with a paper company in Terre Haute, Indiana.

He suggested that the Sutphins look into the possible acquisition of the estate of Dr. Franklin Miles, of Miles Laboratory fame, in Ft. Myers, then a budding area whose principal boast was that it had been chosen as the best place in Florida by Thomas Edison, Henry Ford and Harvey Firestone, who had all acquired estates on the Caloosahatchee River.

The Miles estate was on the same river in a setting that was wildly picturesque and promising. The Sutphins didn't hesitate once they had seen it. They knew this was the perfect place for them.

At the time of the acquisition, it is doubtful Al and Mary had any inkling of the remarkable history of this site. Franklin Miles had first come to Fort Myers in 1906. He fell in love with the town and within a short period of time, owned more than 3,000 acres in Lee County.

One of his first and most important purchases came about on a northbound train as Miles returned to his home in Elkhart, Indiana. He

Henry Ford, Thomas Edison & Harvey Firestone

met a Confederate colonel who owned some landmark property known as Shell House Pointe, eight miles southwest of Fort Myers on the Caloosahatchee River. The colonel told Miles he was anxious to sell because his Southern belle wife had refused to relocate to such a remote, wilderness area.

Doctor Miles was familiar with the famous dwelling that had stood vacant for years. The house itself resembled a French chateau, surrounded by an oyster shell wall, eighteen inches thick, that could withstand an Indian attack. Cattlemen still camped at the abandoned home on the cattle drives that passed through Fort Myers. Local lore had it that the place was haunted by the ghosts of card playing cowboys, felled in a hail of bullets over five-card stud. Such nonsense didn't faze Miles. He shook hands with the soldier, closed the deal, and soon had his family moved to the property.

Miles and his family occupied the spacious 17-room house until 1926 when a fire destroyed it. During those years on the farm, Franklin Miles became instrumental in developing Southwest Florida as an outstanding agricultural area. His techniques revolutionized the methods for cultivating farm land by uniquely adapting to the seasonal weather patterns of Fort Myers. He perfected the art of dry farming in the winter-spring seasons and wet farming in summer and fall.

Dr. Miles died in 1929. His widow lived until 1941, but the condition of the farm greatly deteriorated in her waning years. When Al

Shell House Pointe (1906)

Sutphin appeared on the scene in the fall of 1940, Mrs. Miles had resigned herself to the fact that the time had come to sell her famous estate. A property with a colorful and storied history was about to embark on a new era, one that would prove to be just as unusual and even more entertaining.

Ed Bang, the sports columnist of the *Cleveland News* and an influential figure in Al Sutphin's youth, wrote about this Florida venture:

"While visiting with Al Sutphin at his fabulous Braden-Sutphin Farms at Ft. Myers, I asked Al how this lovely place came into being. Its history is quite interesting.

"When first purchased, the land was literally a jungle, with one tree matted into the other, and a effort was made to save some of them. But eventually it was decided to remove all of the trees and start with the landscaping from scratch.

"...The laying out of the property, landscaping, building of the roads and placing of the shrubbery were under the direct supervision of Al himself, who worked with his own farm labor in fashioning perhaps one of the most beautiful layouts in Florida.

The riverside property in Ft. Myers was purchased in three stages in 1940, and in its uncared for native condition it was a daunting sight. Neglect through the years had allowed the property to take on the look of an overgrown jungle, covered as it was with wild trees and tropical undergrowth.

What came to view, after all the hard work on the banks of the Caloosahatchee, was 45 acres of prime land on which Sutphin proceeded to lay out a road system that branched off a most impressive parkway like en-

In the Beginning...

trance, Palm Tree Road, a wide avenue lined with tall royal palm trees. He also created a blueprint of lots on which buildings of one kind or another would be built in future years. One of his assistants in this labor of love was his son, Jim.

"We had these 20-foot poles, and I would hold the pole while Dad laid out the road and the lots. It was hotter than hot. No shade at all. And my Dad used to say, 'Just think. When you grow up, you can say I helped plant all these trees. At the age of eleven or twelve, I couldn't have cared less. But it was pretty remarkable. The pines were only about three feet tall when we put them in, lined each side of the road, and, of course, the perimeter of the property. Hundreds of Australian pines. They grew to full height. Probably fifty to sixty feet high."

Out of the difficult beginning years, though, the Fort Myers Farm developed into something much more than a family compound. Buildings sprang up everywhere, but the Champ was never satisfied. He continually added new improvements, new buildings, new amenities. As it had been in his creation of the Cleveland Arena, Sutphin gloried in bringing his concepts into reality, but in Florida his vision kept widening in scope. Ultimately, there were twelve houses and fifteen apartments, as well as a community building called the Casino, which served as a common dining hall and a recreation center.

Ernie Sutphen

One of the Farm's major buildings was the residence for Al and Mary to share, and, in true Sutphin tradition, it was built with two wings. One provided living quarters for Al and the other contained an apartment for Mary. The two were linked by a comfortable breezeway. This central house, headquarters of the Caloosahatchee River estate, was low and rambling, of white stucco, modest in its dimensions and homey in its furnishings. Mary saw to that. Al built the roost, but Mary ruled it. It shouldn't be surprising that their home, like all the other buildings on the farm, sported a bright red trim, the authentic Sutphin touch.

Never a year passed without some visible improvement to the Fort Myers Farm. The entrance roadway, Palm Tree Road, was paved in the mid-50's, and the Gate House was built at the entrance where incoming guests were welcomed and guided to their quarters.

There were several small cottages behind the Gate House, and one served as a home for Grandpa Sutphen. It was in keeping with the unassuming nature of this man that he would elect to live away from the main flow of the activity on the Farm. It wasn't that he stayed aloof, but it was typically his choice to stay in the background of his son's frenetic public and private life. He was openly proud of Al's success, ready with advice when it was asked, but he was never one to interfere.

Carlton Ernest "Ernie" Sutphen was a popular grandfather who loved children and manifested that love in many gentle, unassuming ways.

He had a special talent for mimicking the calls and songs of many kinds of birds, one he nurtured all his life. The move to Florida widened his range, of course, and when he practiced on the porch of his house, the trills and whistles brought appreciative smiles to the faces of family and guests.

The estate is thought to have been given its identity as a "farm" during the war years. Gasoline was rationed and it was advantageous, in any bid for a larger allotment of fuel, for an enterprise to somehow contribute to the war effort. Working farms were included in that category, and an earnest effort was made to grow crops of one kind or another on the property. Sixteen acres were set aside as a citrus grove to produce oranges and grapefruit each year to help to cover the cost of the operation. But the fruit was not high in quality and the Farm itself was off the beaten track, unable to attract substantial roadside sales.

Dinner on the Farm (1955)

Even if sale of fruit grown on the Farm failed to defray the property's operating costs, it did serve the cause. Hundreds of bushels were sent north each year for gifts to the Braden-Sutphin salesmen and their accounts.

The development of the Fort Myers property was steady but slow during the 1940's. The sheer physical necessity of clearing the land and making it ready for use was time consuming, but the major factor was that Al Sutphin was at his busiest elsewhere during that decade with Braden-Sutphin Ink , the Arena and the Barons. Any one of those enterprises would keep an ordinary man busy around the clock, but Al also found time for travel abroad and myriad social and charitable enterprises. With all his distractions, Florida kept a firm grip on his affection.

The 1950's was most eventful for the Farm. The demands of the Arena and the hockey team were behind him, and Al was free to push the Florida dream. Most of the buildings on the Farm were built in that period. It was a golden age, not only of development, but for the Farm to ascend to its place as the center of Sutphin family life and social outreach.

Employees of Braden-Sutphin shared in the joys of Fort Myers, just as Al had planned. Each was offered a 10-day vacation in one of the cottages, all expenses paid.

As guests, however, the ink company personnel were distinctly in the minority. Sutphin had friends in all walks of life, and winter invitations to share the good life on the banks of the Caloosahatchee River

Hostess Mary

invariably brought a heavy response. As many as 75 guests enjoyed the hospitality of Al and Mary at one time. Added to the family members and employees, it meant that 100 persons or more could be counted down on the farm.

The logistical problems were many and expensive, but they were met head-on without any visible distress. Besides adequate lodging, food and transportation, the host family also supplied entertainment. In meeting those challenges, Mary Sutphin may have been the busiest woman in Florida but there was never any question that, for all the work and responsibility, she enjoyed the excitement of the Farm.

From the earliest days of their marriage, Al and Mary took great pleasure in the roles of host and hostess. This made for a fortuitous situation because a born salesman like Al Sutphin could not have lived a reclusive life.

Long before the Florida Farm, Al and Mary probably had the busiest social life of any family on Berkshire Road, most of it unplanned and spontaneous, thanks to the Champ's weakness for offhand invitations to friends, neighbors, associates, clients, and even strangers. But he never was able to create a social crisis that Mary couldn't handle.

"My mother was always in the thick of things," marveled Jimmy Sutphin. "and when a friend of dad's one time said to him, 'Al, how do you get Mary to do all the things she does?", my Dad's answer was, 'Charlie, there isn't a husband in the world with enough on the ball to get his wife to do something that she doesn't want to do. Believe me, Mary loves entertaining!

"I must say, though, she was not a typical wife of a salesman. One time when they were entertaining clients of my Dad at home, Mother put out some playing cards that said 'Cleveland Printing Ink' on them. Dad laughed and said, 'Well, its certainly nice of you to advertise our competitor to our printer friends.'"

It was no ordinary vacation resort that the Sutphins created in Fort Myers. The palm trees and the singing waters of the Caloosahatchee River were great stage props, but there had to be an awful lot of hard work and expert management, not to mention cold cash, behind the semi-tropical curtain.

Ruth Galvin

It was Mary who got the good times on the Farm stirring every day by rising at dawn and driving into town to pick up the day workers and drive them to the Farm for a busy day's work. And it was Mary who chauffeured the same staff of helpers back to their homes in Fort Myers at sundown.

Before the Farm developed its own facilities, the Sutphins used to take all of their guests to the Fort Myers Country Club for special dinners, usually on the weekend. Their needs were met by the club's hostess, Ruth Galvin, and her husband, Charles Galvin, the club manager. Mrs. Galvin had a strong background in the restaurant field with the Schraft Restaurant chain for 20 years.

Sutphin, a demanding customer, was properly impressed by Mrs. Galvin's credentials and professionalism. As the pressure of so many guests at the Farm mounted, he turned to Mrs. Galvin for a solution when he heard that she and her husband were quitting the country club in May of 1953.

Mrs. Galvin hedged when Sutphin made his offer, but finally acquiesced with the understanding that it would be nothing more than a part-time position. She made it clear that she wanted no part of a long-term arrangement. On that basis, she spent the following year straightening out the food-and-drink operation at the Farm. After that the arrangement continued on a strictly temporary basis.

In the beginning, Al Sutphin suggested that Mrs. Galvin drop the formalities.

"Call me Al," he said. "And my wife will be Mary to you."

Mrs. Galvin shook her head. She was strong on employer-employee propriety.

"Sorry," she said. "You'll be Mr. Sutphin and she will be Mrs. Sutphin. And I'll be Mrs. Galvin."

On this businesslike basis was the relationship initiated in December,

1953. It was one of signal success. Mrs. Galvin's background and expertise were called into full play by the assignment. And no matter how urgent, unexpected, or outrageous the demands of the day in the Fort Myers com-

Ray Stoney

mune, she met them all head on with assurance and effectiveness.

Alberta's husband, Ray Stoney, had been pressed into service as the manager of the Farm in its foundling years, and acted in that capacity for 10 years. Eventually, and no doubt with a sigh of relief, he transferred to a sales position at Braden-Sutphin Ink and a highly successful career in that capacity.

Al Sutphin soon asked Mrs. Galvin to take on a widened responsibility by assuming management of the overall Farm. She agreed. At her command was a small staff that included Ruth Knight, Mary Bailey and a strapping young man named Jack Gibson. Hired in 1952 as a carpenter's helper, Gibson soon proved to be a valuable and trusted aid to Sutphin. Eventually, the Champ put him in charge of maintaining the sprawling 45 acres of homes and citrus groves. Gibson was an indispensable and integral part of the Farm activity.

Gibson, who stayed on as Farm manager until 1989, made a major contribution to the property when he designed and built a seawall along the river front with the help of Bill and Rob Leitch, two of the Champ's grandsons. It was a substantial undertaking, extending some 2,250 feet along the Caloosahatchee. Gibson estimated that the construction, between 1973 and 1975, required the placement of some 250,000 tons of rocks and boulders.

As for Mrs. Galvin herself, the "temporary" job in Al Sutphin's Shangri-La actually lasted 24 years, and she never complained of a dull moment at any time in almost a quarter-century!

Many of Sutphin's colleagues, employees and friends found themselves immortalized in a modest way by the names given to houses on the Farm. One of the houses, for example, was named the Stein House after Norbert Stein, Sutphin's aide and the publicist of the Cleveland Arena, later its manager.

The building called the Casino also served as the dining room. It was a favorite gathering place at all hours and the setting for the many special programs that Al and Mary dreamed up for their guests.

The gin rummy game would begin just as soon as the dishes were cleared from the tables. Al liked to sit in the same seat every night, his back to the window. Paul Brown, another regular, also had his favorite seat. The two of them, otherwise among the most genial of men, became intense rivals once the deck was shuffled and the first cards dealt. Fun was fun, but winning was everything.

The Sutphin boys who played on Paul Brown's team in the shuffleboard tournaments remember how important it was to turn in good performances for the Coach. His competitiveness simply would not tolerate shabby play.

Fun and games were the order of the day at the Farm, but it was a demanding routine that in any other organization would have required the services of a full time recreation supervisor. But the Champ was his own director of social activities.

The Champ & Paul Brown

The guests usually poured into Fort Myers on a Monday morning and stayed 10 days. There was a party every week and special events every day and night. Food and beverages were supplied. Machines at the Pool House offered free soft drinks. There was never any expense for the guests.

The last Monday night of the guests' stay was traditionally known as Poem Night. At that affair, held in The Casino, everyone was called on to recite an original poem relating to their experience in Fort Myers. Poem Night had its beginning with a simple gesture of thanks to Al and Mary expressed by Joe and Helen Gideon, perennial winter guests. Instead of writing the usual note of thanks, these two literate souls wrote their appreciation in poem form and requested the Champ to read it at the farewell party. Being the showman that he was, Sutphin immediately saw the possibilities and announced that, henceforth, all guests would be required to follow suit and "perform" the last night of their stay.

That last evening evolved into a major production, a stunning affair not to be taken lightly. Normal casual attire was set aside for suits and fancy dresses. It was first class all the way.

Al and Mary came up with one of the most amusing offerings on the Farm's entertainment program when they appeared as a comedy team in a takeoff of the old Gallagher & Sheen vaudeville routine.

Mary Sutphin would dress up as Mr. Gallagher, wearing a mustache, suit and derby. Al would take the part of Mr. Sheen. The two of them would sing comedy lyrics about their guests' stay that always convulsed their audience. There were skits written, directed, and acted in by all members of the Sutphin family.

Poem Night (1956)

Norbert Stein never failed to capture everyone's attention with his zany skits that included American League umpire Bill Summers, Paul Brown, and son-in-law, Ray Stoney.

And no farewell gathering was complete without awards of all kinds to various guests. Special recognition was given to the worst golfer; the shortest marriage, the strangest suntan and other dubious achievements. But no doubt, the Bull Throwing Trophy was the most coveted citation. It was presented to that person who most exaggerated his accomplishments while fishing, golfing, shuffle boarding or at the gin table. The winner's name was engraved on a brass plaque as a lasting remembrance.

The pomp and circumstance of Poem Night continued for many years. In fact, two leather bound scrapbooks were filled to capacity with the poetic creations of hundreds of friends as a fitting testimonial to the fun, the family and the Farm.

There was a serious side to the Fort Myers Farm as well. Al spent many productive hours in his office (wherever that happened to be at the time) tending to the affairs of Braden-Sutphin and other business interests. He was never far away from a Dictaphone machine and the telephone.

Meanwhile, the retirement complex that Al had visualized on the Farm gradually was taking shape. The office building was followed by the Brinson House, the Dubuc House, the Cape Cod House (to be shared by Al and Mary), the Robishaw House, the Grundman House, the Gideon House, the Stoney House and the Reay House.

Sutphin was fearful that the years would separate him from the old friends and employees that he had come to love. The commune on the Farm would solidify old relationships and keep cherished ones together in the silver years.

"Dad's idea," said Cal, "was that if you spend nearly a lifetime working with individuals, why should they all go their separate ways upon retiring?"

Sutphin was a prominent member of the Fort Myers Country Club, and, in fact, bought a half dozen memberships in the club every year so his guests wouldn't have to pay for their golfing rounds.

In the club's modest early years, when Al and his winter crowd con-tributed a hefty share of the golf club's total annual revenues, this arrangement was heartily welcomed. Later, after a generation of prosperity and expansion, some of the regular members objected to the long-standing special courtesies for Braden-Sutphin Farm guests. Al was understandably miffed and word soon circulated that Sutphin was mulling over the prospects of buying the entire Fort Myers Country Club, leaving the other members out in the cold. Coming from anyone else, this would have been a

"Gallagher & Sheen"

hollow threat, but the Fort Myers crowd was well aware of Sutphin's repu-tation for making impossible deals look easy. The controversy quietly faded away and Farm guests continued to enjoy golf at the club.

Father Reardon, the Irish pastor of St. Francis Xavier Church in Fort Myers, was familiar with Al's Sutphin's take-charge techniques. The Champ didn't attend Mass often at St. Ann's Church in Cleveland Heights, but he frequently escorted Mary Sutphin to church in Fort Myers. It must have been that Father Reardon sometimes tested Al's patience with lengthy homi-lies because Al made it a practice, the first Sunday in town, to seek out the priest and hand him a check for $500.

What made the check a bit different from most was that it was always post-dated, not negotiable until a future date, say three Sundays hence, when Al would be leaving on his northward journey to Cleveland.

"Anytime you talk over ten minutes," he explained to Father Reardon, "I'm canceling the check."

Jim Sutphin remembers that check technique well.

Father Reardon, he recalls, was "a great big Irish priest, about 6 feet 4 inches tall. Maybe he was really shorter than that, but at that time in my life, he was terribly tall."

"My dad used to love to sit in the front row at church and kept look-ing at his watch. And I guarantee you, Father Reardon never ever spoke over nine minutes. He wasn't taking any chances!"

Overleaf: The "honeymooners" in Germany, Mary proudly displays her ponyskin coat!

CHAPTER THIRTEEN

SUTPHIN'S TRAVELS

Al Sutphin was a restless sort who not only seemed to be forever afoot on the domestic plains but whose trips to foreign lands were so numerous they occasioned no more surprise within the family than a jaunt to the corner deli for a quart of milk would have aroused in another household.

There is no authoritative final tally on just how many trips he made overseas. One count says 17; another claims 24. What is not disputed is that travel held an endless fascination for Sutphin throughout his life.

The Champ's peregrinations began involuntarily at an early age when his army outfit was dispatched to the World War I battlefields in France. There, through the smoke of conflict, he caught a glimpse of a wider world and it so aroused his curiosity about foreign countries that he thirsted after the sight of new places for all the years to come.

It wasn't long after that first World War, as a matter of record, that young Sutphin undertook his second journey abroad. That one was a dual delight because his companion was his bride, Mary Hoynes, and the trip to Europe in 1922 was their honeymoon.

The young couple had a private audience with the pope, which anyone who knew Mary Hoynes would have predicted as a certainty on the agenda.

"This (audience) was called 'private,'" Al explained later, "because there were only 400 of us present."

Mary and Al had two subsequent visits with the Holy Father, meeting with Pope Pius XII at his summer residence, Castle Con Dolpho, in 1952 and then in 1960 with Pope John XXIII, at the Vatican.

Another honeymoon highlight that he liked to talk about in later years arose out of the couple's visit to the city of Munich.

Unaware of the presence of Adolph Hitler in that romantic German city, or the unrest there that would eventually take the form of Nazism, the happy Sutphins went shopping. Their timing couldn't have been better because all of postwar Germany at the time was in the throes of the worst inflation the country ever has known.

"It was in Munich, on our honeymoon," Sutphin later wrote, "that

Al & Mary with Pope John XXII ... (1960)

I bought your Mother a fur coat for 93 million marks." He hastened to explain that an American dollar at that point was worth 93,000 marks.

He also took his bride to the French countryside where he had been stationed during World War I. The war itself was so recent that he was able to introduce Mary to many of the French villagers and farmers that he had come to know during his time of service.

It was the first of many pilgrimages to France, his favorite destination, but as he grew older, his travel scope gradually widened to take in the remainder of Europe, the lands of the Middle East, and eventually, the Orient.

Mary Sutphin accompanied him on several later trips, including one in 1959-60 that spanned the globe, but most of the time she was content to anchor the home base, and care for the family.

Only two years after the honeymoon, Al returned to Paris for the Olympic Games, a glamorous part of his athletic fantasies since boyhood. He so enjoyed the 1924 Games in Paris that attendance at following Olympics became a regular duty.

He was in the stands in Antwerp, Belgium, for the 1928 games, and he saw the 1932 games in Los Angeles, but missed the Berlin games in 1936 because he was so deeply involved in construction of the Arena. World War II canceled the games, of course, and it was not until 1948, in London, that he could resume attendance. In 1952 he went to Helsinki, this time taking his two sons with him.

The Olympics: 1932 (Los Angeles)   *The Olympics: 1948 (London)*

"We had a great time," Jim remembered. "We rented an apartment from a Finnish family. They moved out for the two weeks, and we moved in."

The 1952 Olympic games were among the best and most exciting, especially to the fans from Cleveland. They had a fellow-townsman to cheer on, Harrison Dillard, onetime track star from Baldwin-Wallace College.

Dillard failed to qualify for the 110-meter high hurdle race in the 1948 games, but went on to win the 100-meter competition and staged a comeback in the high hurdles in Helsinki winning the race handily.

The three Sutphins went on to Copenhagen from Helsinki. When they arrived, the elder Sutphin clapped his hands at the sight of the North Sea and announced that he and his two sons were about to go swimming. It was a unilateral decision that drew a loud but futile protest from the boys.

"I looked around and couldn't see anybody else swimming," Jim said, "but my dad, who was a very hardy soul, said, 'We're going to go swimming in the North Sea,' and that was that. We went swimming. Now I know why they call it the North Sea!"

For Sutphin, travel was serious business. Every trip was meticulously planned in advance, with every conceivable need anticipated. A trip was like a military expedition with the destination clearly in mind,

Harrison Dillard at Helsinki

the travel routes carefully planned and all logistical demands satisfied. An integral part of this preparation was research. Al read everything available about the area he planned to visit and often ended up with local knowledge that rivaled professional guides and even the natives themselves.

Another hallmark of Sutphin's travels through foreign lands was an overwhelming urge to share the pleasures and experiences he encountered with the folks back home, and he adopted a perennial practice of recording his impressions and reflections in a virtual daily journal.

A minor difficulty in the beginning was that he hated to write. It was too slow and laborious, and not at all in keeping with his pace. As a businessman, he was used to having a secretary ease the burden of communication through shorthand or the use of the dictaphone machine, a crude but effective predecessor of modern recording devices. And the machine had the advantage of being a lot more portable than a secretary.

Whenever he was at sea or in foreign lands, his dictaphone machine was always close at hand. He would fill cylinder after cylinder with his primitive version of voice mail, and the tubes carrying his recordings would be mailed to his secretary at Braden-Sutphin, Jane McManamon. It was her job to transcribe the Sutphin travel diary, no easy task considering all the names of foreign places and foreign people, and then mimeograph the dispatches and mail copies by the hundreds to the extensive mailing list of family, friends and business associates, as well as customers. This travel diary was about as stern a test of secretarial skill, ingenuity and patience as any employer could devise.

Not surprisingly, the McManamons, Jane and Tom, became as much a part of the Sutphin family, in time, as the blood relatives, thanks to their special roles in the family's business activities.

When Tom McManamon had gone overseas on army duty in 1943, his wife went to work at Braden-Sutphin for Norbert Stein, long-time right-hand man to Sutphin, and member of a small coterie of associates whom the Champ came to depend on through the years.

Upon McManamon's return to civilian status at war's end, he was hired by Sports Services to run concessions in the Cleveland Arena. In 1949, he transferred to the Braden-Sutphin Ink Company to serve as office manager. Eventually, Tom McManamon rose to Chairman of the Board and served in that capacity until his death in 1994. Through the years, the McManamons became far more than employees. Sutphin called the McManamon offspring his "grandchildren."

The McManamons

Jane was not the only member of the McManamon family to be involved in Al Sutphin's travels. When the Champ undertook one of his frequent tours of Europe, he liked to ride in his own automobile, and he wanted it driven by someone he trusted. He was a notoriously nervous passenger. Native drivers he had encountered in foreign countries all seemed to have a suicidal flair that kept Sutphin on the edge of his seat. So it was that Tom McManamon was called on over the years occasionally to assume the role of confidante, companion and chauffeur. Of all the important responsibilities that he was entrusted with, none was more demanding than steering Al Sutphin through the narrow, winding streets of European cities and the highways of the foreign countryside.

The Sutphin automobile, whatever the year, usually crossed the ocean with its owner. The favorite was a red Cadillac, in keeping with the Champ's color tradition. He had more than one new automobile repainted his favorite hue before he would drive it down the street.

The war still was recent in the minds of Europeans when, in 1948, the Sutphin entourage rode in a Chrysler convertible with wooden sides and a bright red trim calculated to dazzle the most blasé of onlookers. But on a continent that had only begun to recover from the World War, the glittering Sutphin automobile was an astonishing sight.

"Anybody would think Al Sutphin intended to start an overseas branch of his Arena, considering the attention he managed to attract on a recent trip to Europe," commented the *Cleveland Press* in a September, 1948 edition.

"Sutphin went for a good time, but he just can't help promoting, even on a vacation. And by the time he had finished flashing the continent with his red ties and country club convertible to match, thousands of people from Belgium to Switzerland knew he was there."

Jim Sutphin admires Al's Cadillac...

Whenever the Sutphins car stopped in a town or village, crowds flocked to its side, The sight of the young people always brought out the best in Al Sutphin, and he had gone to Europe prepared to deal with them on the terms he knew they would love best. He would step out of the car and distribute chocolate candy bars to their eager, outstretched hands. On that particular journey, he handed out over a thousand chocolate bars.

But children weren't the only Europeans to share in the beneficence of the Cleveland sportsman. On that same trip, he distributed countless one-dollar bills to waiters, bellhops, and, in fact, to anyone whose gaunt, hollow-eyed look told him of past deprivation and suffering.

"They all love dollars," he once sighed. "It's the best thing there is in the world today." If so, his Chrysler convertible may have been no lower in the public rating than second place.

"No one in Europe had seen anything like it," he said. "In Belgium, France, Holland, Germany and Switzerland, when I'd park the thing in front of a restaurant, I'd have to fight my way out of the place to get back in the car. One place in Germany, fully a thousand people surrounded the auto. The carpenters were especially interested. They wanted to know how the wood could be held together without nails!"

It was almost as true in 1948 as it is today that a traveler anywhere in this steadily shrinking world was never far from home. The spidery

The 1948 Cleveland Indians ... World Champs!

antennae of modern communications have a way of seeking us out in the most unlikely places, as they did Al Sutphin during his travels that year..

For the Champ, every trip had its own personality and a distinct set of qualifications for remembrance.

Some people remember 1948 as the year in which Harry S. Truman was elected President of the United States. Fellow townsmen of Al Sutphin will think of 1948 mainly as the year the Cleveland Indians won the pennant and the World Series.

Sutphin, in a letter to his old friend Ed McAuley of the *Cleveland Press*, marveled over the effect that the winning ways of the Indians was having on that part of the world.

"Although I have visited Europe many times, this visit is the first time that I heard baseball ever discussed on the boulevards in the various capitals of the world.

"For the first time, visiting Americans were talking about the two hectic races being staged in the American and National leagues.

Bill Veeck

European sports promoters that I visited were simply bewildered by the terrific gate receipts that baseball is drawing this year in America, and almost all of them knew of Bill Veeck's tremendous success.

"If they knew Bill Veeck, they wouldn't be so surprised.

"When a man's fame can spread all the way to Europe, he really has accomplished miracles. Inasmuch as you are one of the few (very few) sentimentalists left in sports...I should like to relate the following incident.

"While driving through Alsace Lorraine on my way to the Rhine, we chose to drive into the town of Domremy, the birthplace and childhood of Joan de Arc. It was about eight o'clock in the evening. The sun was setting on this lovely village, and I had the radio turned on to a symphony that was being broadcast to our American boys in the Occupation Zone.

"Being after visiting hours, the home (of Joan de Arc) was locked up, but on our stopping the car, the old lady who was keeper of the keys came hurrying across the street and, with typical French courtesy, opened Joan de Arc's house to us, led us through the garden through which a beautiful small stream flowed, and led us also into the pitifully poor, rather dilapidated church where Joan de Arc worshipped.

"The setting of all this, along with the glories of a setting sun and simple villagers who had gathered, caused a great feeling of awe and inspired humility as we returned to the car and the symphony. As I turned on the motor, the symphony had become a raucous broadcast of a ball game between the Yankees and the Boston Red Sox...

"Here we were in the lap of the gods, in the township of tradition and history, and BASEBALL was paramount even here!"

The Champ himself was never far from baseball, whether in Cleveland or in Domremy. It had been his favorite sport in the days of his youth and it always remained close to his heart. It was rumored in the Cleveland sports pages that, following the departure of Bill Veeck, Sutphin might buy the Indians. Sutphin did own stock in the club at one time and there is the likelihood that he would have gotten more involved with the club had he not been so weighed down by his other responsibilities.

Regrettably for Cleveland, the circumstances would not allow the Champ to take the plunge into major league baseball. Without someone of Sutphin's caliber to follow Veeck's act, the Indians faded into decades of mediocrity, finally returning to glory with a vengeance in the 1990's.

Al proudly escorts Mary, Jane, Carolyn & Alberta
on the Queen Elizabeth (1948)

His many journeys to the distant ports of the world satisfied more than Al Sutphin's natural curiosity about places beyond the horizon. When it came to sustenance, as in other areas, Sutphin had a unique approach and he was not a man whose appetite was to be trifled with. While he followed an irregular pattern of eating—hardly ever touching food until mid-afternoon—he was very particular about what he ate. One way or another, the results had a way of showing up quickly in his girth.

Travel, of course, exposed his appetite to new temptations and exotic delights that overcame the firmest of human resolve. The Champ was naturally hefty in physique and had to combat the temptations of the table at all times, especially in the liberated atmosphere of a luxury liner or a gourmet's paradise like Paris.

What would have undermined any person's resistance were the prices on the bill of fare in the restaurants of the Europe, especially during the depression and postwar years. Even he, always the free-handed spender, found it hard to believe what money could buy in those unstable years.

On his 1948 trip, " most of our meals in rural France were about a

dollar a person, and marvelous meals," he wrote. "Rooms at night ONE
DOLLAR A PERSON."

The price scale was different in the big city, of course.

"Here in Paris," he went on, "we are paying $2.25 a person for rooms;
lunch about a dollar. Our dinner is about $2.50 — and what a dinner!"

He went on to itemize the typical $2.50 dinner in Paris: hors
d'oeuvres, soup, petite fish with sauce, steak and chicken, salad, two veg-
etables, coffee (very strong - add hot milk) or tea, ice cream covered
with strawberries or raspberries.

"Butter is extra. The bread divine. Betz and Reiser are splitting a
bottle of wine with each meal ($1.00 a bottle).

"Believe it or not, we were getting these kinds of meals in rural
France for $1 a person (300 francs to the dollar)."

Writing from Deauville on the French Coast, Al noted:

"This is the Miami Beach, the Palm Beach, or Bar Harbor of France.
Hotels a la White Sulphur Springs, tops in expense. Slept our first night
here. Rooms $3.00 a person, meals $3.00 a person. The only expensive
place so far."

It was another world, another time, and Al Sutphin knew it well for
the bargain it was. But cost never was the deciding factor in his approach to life. Money was only useful as the means to a pleasant end,
and when money was plentiful—as it was—pleasure was assured.

All things considered, the Champ's decision to have somebody like
Tom McManamon at the wheel of his car during his journeys across Europe emerged as pure wisdom. What Al Sutphin considered a vacation
would have made others cringe, but he had his own concept of what
constituted work and play, and he enjoyed the mixture whether at home
or abroad.

Writing from shipboard, he marveled at his own vacation formula:

"Truly, your father has always known how to relax on ships," he
wrote, "and yet I am following the usual custom of working every morning from seven o'clock until lunch or one o'clock. Started out on this
trip only working until breakfast hour, but that didn't last long. Along
came the sales reports, the checking of payrolls... We now have been on
board for twelve weeks and am completing my 96th letter...to the sales
organization, the factory, and to many, many customers. Have the
dictaphone with me, and spend each morning of six hours, exactly as I
would have at home ..."

The automobile simplified their travel problem in a gratifying way, allowing them to visit places on back streets and remote highways that would not have been accessible otherwise. But when the Sutphin party said farewell to France and headed for England, their slick convertible became a problem. Sutphin told the story:

The Queen Elizabeth

"We sailed to France out of Le Havre...stood on the dock and watched a giant crane swing the lovely Chrysler high into the air and drop it gently into the hold of the boat. Came the early morning at the docks at Southampton and our boat was tied with a thousand guy ropes to the pier and we had gone through the herded experience, along with hundreds of people going through immigration and then through customs—and English customs are tough—when it is discovered we are tied to a dock that does not have a crane that can lift a car weighting 4,500 pounds! What to do? They don't know.

"They (the English) claimed the 'Dumb French at Le Havre' should have known that the Southampton Dock for this steamship line couldn't handle this car ....Only thing to do was to go back to France and come back to England on another boat....What a dilemma!

"... It was finally decided to move the boat to another dock. But by that time the seaman were gone. The day's work was done by Her Majesty's Navy.

"However, there are some good scouts among the officials, and then we had a number of Greenbacks with the eagles simply screaming to be let out into the English sunlight. AND THEY MOVED THAT GREAT BOAT to another dock and swung our Monster unto English soil ...!"

There was no such thing as a dull trip anywhere in Al Sutphin's view, but some were more fun than others.

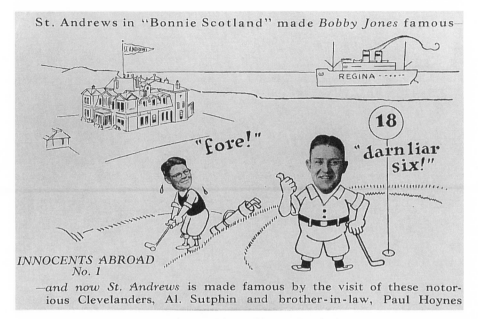

At St. Andrews, Al Sutphin & Paul Hoynes

A frequent traveling companion was his brother-in-law, Paul Hoynes. Of all their overseas journeys, the one they liked to talk about most was the trip that almost ended before it got started.

Taking them from New York to Europe was the majestic *Queen Elizabeth*, a ship that waits for no commoner.

Al and Paul somehow were delayed on their way to the dock in New York. When they arrived at water's edge, it was to see the *Queen Elizabeth* already riding the harbor waters, moving out to sea.

Lesser men might have been discouraged, but the two Clevelanders, in high spirits, hired a boat to take them in pursuit of the ship they had missed. After an exciting sea chase, they finally caught up with the British liner, whose captain, no doubt in admiration of such a show of American tenacity, had a rope ladder dropped down the side of the vessel and welcomed them to climb aboard!

Another voyage that had a most interesting beginning was the one that Al and Mary took in 1960. This was the BIG trip; the one that would take the two of them all around the world.

Young Cal accompanied Al and Mary to New York City. After an overnight stay in the Abbey Hotel, the three were supposed to drive to the pier in Hoboken where the senior Sutphins would board the *President Polk* of the U. S. President's Line.

The Champ noted in his daily travel report to the folks back home that "on Thursday, March 3rd, the day before sailing, your Mother blew into New York to join me on our World Cruise."

"And 'blew,'" he added, "is the correct word, inasmuch as she brought the worst snow storm and wind storm that New York has experienced in 17 years. A howling wind...shook the windows, and offered some misgivings about heading out into the cold Atlantic the following day.

"It must be remembered that the *President Polk* is a very small vessel. Only 9,000 tons, just one-tenth the tonnage of the *Queen Elizabeth* on which I am accustomed to traveling. The *Queen Elizabeth* weighs slightly more than 90,000 tons!"

The ferocious storm delayed the loading of the ship's cargo, causing a full day's postponement of the departure a full day.

"Cal drove us to the boat, which sailed from Jersey City, and it was amazing how the dear boy was able to remember his way to the pier at night..."

It seems that Cal was just as amazed. His recollection of the drive through the streets covered with heavy drifts with the car buffeted by lashing winds was one of a lingering horror as he groped his way against a background of back seat gasps and groans. "But we made it to the ship on time," said Cal.

Al and Mary had serious misgivings about their dream trip when they boarded the *President Polk*.

"But we did sail into high seas," he wrote, "and to our great surprise the little ship, heavily loaded with cargo, rode magnificently. And in spite of the weather, we had no difficulty in visiting the dining room for each meal."

The raging seas quickly calmed and the stout little ocean liner demonstrated its seaworthiness and comfort, earning the Sutphin's complete affection.

It was on that trip that Al Sutphin's travel letters to his friends reached their full literary flower. Instead of one or two countries as subjects for his commentary, the 1960 voyage offered the Champ the whole world—or much of it, anyway—as fodder for his ruminations. Where on other trips he had to confine himself to the narrow observations of a gourmet, he could

Al & Mary in the Holy Land

now afford to play the expansive role of gourmand. This was his travel banquet, and he was determined to share its delights with everybody.

A small hint as to the literary burden that the Champ assumed is to be found in the fact that he and Mary took along some 4,000 Christmas cards they had received the previous holiday season and which they had not had the time to read individually. They also took bundles of postcards supplemented by cards they bought in foreign ports—6,000 in all, mailed from Japan, Egypt and Italy to an army of relatives and friends.

It was not surprising that their world tour itinerary included Rome and all of the Holy Land, precious destinations for Mary Sutphin. And one of the things that made the stopover in the Eternal City even more enjoyable for both Sutphins was that, in Al's words, they were "royally entertained" there by a former Clevelander, Brother Theophane of the Holy Cross Order, close friend of Paul and Dennis Hoynes. Sutphin often reminisced about that stopover in Rome.

"Brother Theophane gave us the opportunity of visiting many, many places that we had never been privileged to see on previous visits," he wrote to his children. "Included in this was a very marvelous visitation to the Papal Gardens, the private sanctuary of the Pope. Very few people are offered this rare privilege.

"When leaving Rome, I left Brother a sizable check to be used for...the new American College they were building in Rome....Although I had many letters from Brother, he really never mentioned how the money was used, but told me that we had a surprise in store when we came back to Rome in 1960.

"On our arrival this time, Brother gave a magnificent dinner at the college for your Mother and me, and then gave your father his greatest thrill of a lifetime. The Brother had begged considerable marble—in fact, a lot of marble—from the Italian friend who had marble quarries, and used our money to build my greatest thrill. Brother unveiled a most beautiful fountain, all in marble, at the entrance of the college grounds, which carried the inscription:

The Al Sutphin Memorial Fountain.

"In a city 3,000 years old," wrote the pleased honoree, "this fountain is the first 'Protestant Fountain' in the history of Rome to Brother Theophane's knowledge or mine."

The visit to Rome was an unqualified success. A devout Muslim visiting Mecca for the first time could not have been more visibly stirred than was Mary Sutphin in the Holy City. She reveled in the sights and of the capital of Catholicism, and her husband took vicarious pleasure in her delight. It inspired him to write the following self-examination of his own religious feelings:

"All of our Gang know my sentiment concerning religion. Personally, I will perhaps never concern myself too much as to the manner a man takes to reach heaven, be it via the pomp and display of the Catholic church, the simple ritual of Protestantism, or via the Synagogue.

"All roads leading to the Pearly Gates look the same, and I shall continue my own peculiar religion, namely, that of trying to make the lives of friends, associates, and others I come in contact with, just a little happier.

"Considering the great amount of money that I have made for myself, and others, and having retained relatively so little of the great total earned, might be living proof of my actually and honestly living my type of religion.
And sincerely hope that those who know me best will think so too.

"Rome ... Rome ... the city that gave me (the heathen) the five happiest days of my life, simply because Rome gave Mary Sutphin the five happiest days of her life.

"God, If I could only have her faith!"

When they arrived in Lebanon, he pointed out the majority of the population was Catholic, "and your mother is very happy again."

The Champ had a weakness for diving into any famous body of water that he came across in his travels, so it was not surprising when he decided to have a swim in the Mediterranean before leaving Beirut.

As he padded across the hotel lobby in his swim togs and bathrobe, looking forward to the dip, the elevator operator, a small boy, laughed out loud. In further expression of disbelief, he followed Al to the water's edge.

"He had already scrutinized my gray hair and portly figure," Sutphin wrote later, "and when I entered the water, I understood his mirth. The water was colder than ice, and even though I would like to have climbed out, I did not dare under the eyes of the small boy! (He) was amazed. He did not note that I was turning blue!"

It stood to reason that the Al Sutphin who so loved cold air, air conditioning in automobiles in mid-winter, who slept on his screened-in porch when the temperatures were below freezing, would be dismayed by the heat of Egypt. And he was.

He wrote with a desperate pen of desert travel in a "God-awful" Chevrolet with a pair of hapless guides.

"We had six separate breakdowns on the journey," he wrote, "and if we closed the windows of the car, we sweltered and died with heat. If we opened the windows, the flies attacked us by the hundreds. Personally I always thought it was the Egyptians who drove the British from Egypt. Now I know it was the flies."

The Champ noted that he and Mary had met a number of celebrities on their globe-girdling journey.

"I had a long, long talk with Jack Benny in the Peninsula Hotel in Hong Kong," he wrote. "I said, 'Hello, Jack' and he said, 'Hello,' right back."

Another time, Gene Kelly was at a nearby table in a small restaurant and Mary wanted to ask Kelly for his autograph.

"But I wouldn't let her. I was afraid he would ask for her telephone number."

Sutphin almost became a movie star himself during the stopover in the King David Hotel in Jerusalem.

Motion picture crews had all but taken over the hotel as they used it as their headquarters during filming of the classic motion picture, *Exodus*.

Mary Sutphin described the scene:

"Directly in the center of the hotel on the street side, there is a large porch beneath which cars can drive in order to deposit passengers....On this porch were great sand bags and actors dressed as British Tommies with machine guns. The cameras were across the street....On the street side, where we had our small room, there was a very narrow balcony. Not one where you could sit and lounge, but one where you could barely stand.

"Your father walked out on the balcony and soon heard great shouting through a megaphone to 'Get the hell out of there!'"

It wasn't until he closed the door leading to the balcony that the shouts died down. Apparently, Kirk Douglas didn't need another co-star and the Sutphins were forced to swelter through the night, shuttered in their room, harassed by the floodlights and noise of the moviemakers. Al did not look back with pleasure on this brush with film immortality.

When the Sutphins arrived in Hong Kong, they found four large passenger ships in port "and women, women pouring out of each ship, all unescorted and on fire looking for bargains. After seeing what goes on in our various ports of call and the antics of the widows," he wrote, "it makes me worry about dying. And I will resent dying very much."

It was in Hong Kong that the Sutphins had a surprise reunion with an old friend from home, and the Champ, never one to overlook the opportunity for a practical joke, made the most of it.

"... One Sunday morning your mother had gone to church in Hong Kong and I was working on the mail just received in my bedroom on the boat. And like all men I was thinking about beautiful women, when there came a rap at my door, and there stood a beautiful one!

"Seventy-seven years old, and still gorgeous: Mrs. James Braden!

You have no idea how pleased I was to see her. Her round-the-world ship was laying alongside.

"She did not stay long inasmuch as she had the widow's urge to hasten to downtown Hong Kong, looking for bargains. But I did make an arrangement by which we would take her to dinner and I would deliver her as a surprise to your mother come the dinner hour.

"Comes evening, I ...brought Mrs. Braden up to my room...tucked her into one of my beds, then went over into your Mother's room, telling her that I had a 'babe' in my room who apparently had too much to drink and I could not get her out.

"You may be sure your Mother hurried over to remedy the situation — and found Mrs. B.!!!

"Boy! Your Mother was really surprised!"

That 1960 trip with Mary Sutphin may have been the most memorable of all the many overseas excursions taken by the Champ. His dispatches home had a lilt and an ebullience that said much.

But there were detectable shadows across those pages as well. Most explicit in its forecast of future decline was Al's New Year's letter from Paris.

"Dear Gang: What a busy year. Plan on going home and to bed for a month.

"New Year's. The hospital discovers diabetes and incurable hip. 'Walk as little as possible,' says the doctor ...

"Wonderful days, exciting, full of pleasure—but exerting, particularly on a hip that doesn't function." (He had injured the hip playing baseball at a picnic at age 50 and it bothered him for the rest of his life, eventually forcing him into a wheel chair.)

There was a happier note in his next dispatch, written as he and Mary prepared to take their leave of his beloved Paris.

"The last days in Paris," he wrote. "Last night a visit to Ciro's, finest restaurant in Paris....A thrill. (When we got the invoice, you could understand why.)

"Never had the lovely Mary shown me so much attention. Perhaps it is because I am becoming more attractive. Or perhaps it is the first time she ever had more than two drinks at any one time. Frankly, it is amazing what a dozen goblets of champagne will accomplish!"

The "Unforgetable" wedding trip, aboard the Queen Mary, 1964 Front row, seated, l. to r., Mary E. Sutphin, Louise Sutphin, Alberta Stoney, Sandy Sutphin, Carolyn Leitch, Jane Leitch. Back row, standing, l. to r., Jim Sutphin, waiter, Ray Stoney, waiter, wine steward, waiter & Cal Sutphin

Al & Mary "Tour" Egypt, 1960

Al, Cal & Jim in Helsinki
(1952)

Team U.S.A. marching in...Helsinki (1952)

The Olympic village, Antwerp, Belgium (1920)

Dan & Paul Hoynes, Al's life-long
friends and brothers-in-law

Al & Tom McManamon
traveling to Europe again!

Al with family & friends on Cal Sutphin's wedding trip
Beer hall, Munich, Germany, July 1964

Overleaf: Braden Sutphin Farms Coat of Arms

CHAPTER FOURTEEN

LIFE ON THE CALOOSAHATCHIE

During the winter months, when Fort Myers and the Braden-Sutphin Farm were at their sunny best, the family estate on the banks of the Caloosahatchie River offered rich diggings for enterprising autograph hunters with its fascinating array of visiting notables from all walks of life. Al and Mary Sutphin had many famous friends and almost all of them, at one time or another, were guests on the Farm.

Prominent among those special friends were the Paul Browns. The Sutphins found them to be kindred souls.

Brown was known to the outside world as the founding coach of the Cleveland Browns and Cincinnati Bengals. Many sports experts contend that he was the greatest football coach of all time, and at the very least belongs among the best mentors and strategists in that sport.

The Browns would have been enthusiastically welcomed in the most exclusive vacation resorts of high society, but they chose to spend their winter months with the Sutphins at Fort Myers for many years.

Sharing the Champ's legendary hospitality were other celebrities, many from the world of sports. They included Bill Summers, chief umpire of the American League; Chicago Blackhawks owner, Bill Tobin; former Indians and White Sox manager, Jimmy Dykes; former mayor Ray Miller; star pitcher Early Wynn; and Don Miller, U. S. Attorney and one of Notre Dame's "Four Horseman."

The illustrious list included also Lou ("The Toe") Groza, Tim Conway of Fisher Foods, Al Lopez, Bob Feller, sports announcer Tom Manning, former Kentucky and Browns head coach, Blanton Collier, and a host of Cleveland newspapermen.

Whoever the guests were, their arrival in Fort Myers was accompanied by proper ceremony and fanfare—an honest-to-goodness musical fanfare, that is, thanks to the Champ's love of the theatrical flare. He would hire the Dunbar High School band to greet the new guests. That full-bodied musical reception invariably took the breath away from first-

Katie & Paul Brown pound out a tune in "The Casino"

time guests. After the salute from the band, they would be escorted to convertibles and given a tour of the city and the Farm.

Sometimes, while the new arrivals were still in a state of shock over the elaborate welcome, Sutphin was not above a practical joke or two. One of his favorite ploys was taking some guests to a screened-in porch furnished only with an ancient dresser and a rickety bed with an old-fashioned pot under it, pretending that this would be their living quarters. The triumph he liked best was assigning that screened-in porch, open to the world, to a honey-mooning couple, leaving them to mull over their predicament.

From arrival to departure, the Farm's guests were confronted with one surprise after another. The Sutphin social pace was without letup. It began early the first morning when the loudspeaker system would explode with the old World War I tune, "Oh, How I Hate to Get Up in the Morning!" jarring all the guests out of their sleep. After that, they were ready for anything, one would suppose. And one would be wrong.

There was, for example, the Farm pet called Chuckles.

Chuckles was a live alligator kept in a pen in the courtyard. Visitors from the North found the animal to be a fascinating sight and Al always went out of his way to direct them to the alligator cage.

But Chuckles came to a sorry end, the victim of some Fort Myers hoodlums. He was wantonly done in one night by some young men from town said to be members of prominent families.

Al sorrowfully went out and bought another alligator whom he named Chuckles II, but the incident bothered him for a long time, probably because it introduced an element of violence which never before had been present on the Farm.

The Champ's escapades made a deep impression on his children. It was, to them, a continuing entertainment as the head of the household blandly set up his friends and guests in one outrageous situation after another. Alberta remembers them well.

"One of Father's practical jokes was providing a guest with a knife and fork that would collapse on use. All of us kids thought that was a riot."

The six children would watch the guest with the trick silverware, anticipating the critical moment of use, and when the knife and fork and spoon folded, so did the Sutphin kids, fully as collapsible as the trick cutlery.

Mary Sutphin seemed to draw as much enjoyment from practical jokes on guests at the Farm as her husband, and

Chuckles

she was just as deeply involved in some of his plots. One of Alberta's favorite was the notorious Chicken Neck Dinner.

During a normal week on the Farm, the Sutphin guests were treated to one outstanding repast after another, and by week's end they had come to expect nothing but the best. They were softened up for the kill, which came with the delivery to the dinner table of a huge platter of chicken necks. The startled guests naturally were too polite to make any critical remarks, but they were always taken aback even as they dutifully took a helping of chicken necks for their plates.

After a somewhat embarrassing silence, the Champ usually would rise and explain to his guests that it had been a bad week for him and that chicken necks were the best he could afford that night. The guests, while perplexed by this sudden turn of events, usually nodded understandingly.

That's when Mary would appear at the table bearing a platter of the savory and delicious chicken parts—the rest of the chickens—and the guests, realizing they had been taken in by Al, would join in an uproarious laugh at themselves.

The most remarkable period of growth and popularity in Fort Myers followed World War II. Al Sutphin's arrival on the scene at that time may be regarded as strictly coincidental, but maybe not. He did much to publicize and popularize the area back home in Ohio.

Not surprisingly, the Sutphins quickly established themselves as participating members of the community. They were not, under the Champ's leadership, to be confused with tourists. Besides his expensive enhancement of the 45-acre property on the banks of the river, Sutphin took a direct interest in all of the city's concerns.

Connie Mack Sr.   *Young Senator Connie Mack III*

The Fort Myers establishment soon became aware of the Sutphin presence, just as it would have been if the city had been targeted by a tropical hurricane. Sutphin's personal flamboyance, his showmanship and unorthodox methods, his stature in the national world of sports and his aggressive local involvement all came together to win him the attention and respect of his new Florida neighbors.

Fort Myers, by that time, had become home to the Sutphins in a very real sense. The sports interests up north had loosened their hold, and while Braden-Sutphin Ink continued to be his principal interest, he was able to keep abreast of its affairs by mail, phone, and personal visits. Florida now claimed his hands-on attention.

Son Cal, like his father, had an intense love of sports as well as a talent for baseball that won him a place on the pitching staff of the Ft. Myers High School team in 1957. Among his friends at Fort Myers High was Cornelius McGillicuddy, Jr., more familiarly known as Connie Mack III, grandson of the major league baseball immortal. Young Connie Mack would later earn his own measure of fame as a United States senator.

Baseball was the major sport of the high school and the city itself. Terry Park in Fort Myers long has served as a spring training site for major league clubs, including the Cleveland Indians in 1940-41, the Pittsburgh Pirates in the 50's and 60's and the Kansas City Royals during the 70's and 80's.

When young Cal began pitching for the high school team, his proud father became almost as much a member of the team as the coaching

Celebrating Al's Birthday

staff. There was hardly a day when he didn't appear at the practice sessions and he took his place as the team's most outspoken booster.

"During the summer," said Cal, "thanks to Dad, I was able to work out with the Indians and got a number of pitching lessons from Mel Harder."

"Dad kept all the team's batting and fielding averages," said Cal. "And he provided three station wagons to transport the players and coaches to all our away games in cities like Naples, Venice, Sarasota, Key West and Fort Pierce. The players eventually named the cars, 'The Red Fleet'."

But what Al Sutphin saw on the playing field of the high school did not please him entirely. For one thing, the traditional school colors were green and white, but he resigned himself to the fact that red, after all, was not everybody's favorite color. What he would not accept, however, was that the team uniforms were old and shabby in appearance. He offered to buy the entire squad new uniforms, but he attached a condition: the uniforms had to have a trace of red somewhere—perhaps the piping on the sleeves or pants. It was a typical Sutphin touch.

One of Cal's most memorable experiences as a pitcher for Fort Myers High occurred in the two game series with the high school team in Key West. The star player of the opposing team was Boog Powell.

Boog Powell

Cal Sutphin "Ballplayer"

"On Friday and Saturday of the Easter weekend in 1958, the 'Red Fleet' rolled from Fort Myers to Key West. We played Boog Powell and his team twice, and the scores were like 14 to 1 and 5 to 0 against us.

"Boog Powell was the best hitter that I have ever seen to this day for a high school student...and it only took him two years to make it to the major leagues with the Baltimore Orioles. One of the few bright spots in our two-day series was when I came in relief and struck out Powell."

One of Sutphin's admirers was Len Harsh, sports editor of the *Fort Myers News-Press*. The Champ was never too busy for Harsh, and was always willing to swap views on sports issues of the day. One day in 1957, Harsh and Sutphin were having just such an informal chat when the owner of the Farm mentioned that he was going to attend the World Series in New York City. He hardly ever missed that blue ribbon classic.

"Are you going to cover the Series?" Sutphin asked.

Harsh said he would not. The paper used the wire service coverage.

"Have you ever been to a World Series?" asked the curious Sutphin.

"Nope," said Harsh, trying not to be wistful.

"Well, Len, you are going to see this one," barked Sutphin. "You're going to be my guest, so don't worry about anything."

In one of his columns years later, Harsh remembered a conversation with the Champ.

"Sutphin was reminiscing just a bit and revealed that the Braden-Sutphin farm has had over 16,000 guests over the 27 years span that Sutphin has been here, including over 600 last winter. Al also said that well over 20 of his personal friends who first came to Fort Myers as guests have since bought property and located here permanently.

Jimmy Dykes

"...That figure of over 16,000 guests represents an outlay of millions of dollars over a 27-year period for food, travel and entertainment and other expenses. Anyone who has ever been a guest of Al knows that it is 'first class' all the way with Sutphin. Sutphin prides himself in that he 'has never taken a dollar out of Fort Myers and Lee County' and he never will ...

"Al Sutphin in our book is not only a fine friend but a real gentleman, a good and a great man. In our private file is every letter that Al Sutphin ever wrote to us and his letters are like the man, interesting, informative and something to remember."

Because Fort Myers was so far outside the orbit of major league sports, except during the spring training period of baseball, the visits to the Farm through the year of so many sports celebrities invariably caught the attention of the city and gave the Farm a glamorous aura.

But no amount of glamour could suppress the Champ's weakness for practical jokes. Nothing was too sacred and nobody too famous to escape his sinister schemes. For example, he had printed some labels that said: "Stolen from the Braden-Sutphin Farm" that were sewed inside the jackets of unwary guests.

One such victim was Jimmy Dykes, then manager of the Chicago White Sox. He had just taken his departure from the Farm after a visit when a Fort Myers police car pulled him over and escorted him to the police station.

There a search brought the label to light, just as Sutphin had told them it would in a well-timed telephone call. Dykes was still protesting loudly when Sutphin showed up to release him. There was loud laughter and general hilarity on all sides, but there is no evidence that the old baseball star joined in the amused reaction.

The moral was that nobody was safe once the Champ's sense of humor got loose.

The Sutphin Farm at Ft. Myers, Florida

The Farm at Ft. Myers

The pool at the Farm, Ft. Myers, Florida

The Stein House at the Sutphin Farm at Ft. Myers, Florida

The "Honeymoon Suite" at the Farm, Ft. Myers, Florida

FLORIDA "FARM" REGULARS

Paul Brown

Lou "The Toe" Groza

Blanton Collier
former Browns head coach

Bob Feller

Mike Garcia

Early Winn

in the center: Don Miller & The other "3 Horseman"
Harry Stuhldreher, Elmer Layden & Jim Crowley

Overleaf: 1948 "City of Champions" Calendar

CHAPTER FIFTEEN

YEAR OF GLORY

Professional sports in Cleveland peaked in the year 1948 as the Cleveland Indians won the pennant and World Series; the Cleveland Browns won the football championship and the Cleveland Barons won the American Hockey League title and the coveted Calder Cup.

It was an emotional high point such as few cities ever have experienced, and the entrepreneurs who had brought about THE successful sweep were the toast of the town. Al Sutphin, the senior member of the triumphant triumvirate, admittedly had settled for a lesser prize with his Barons, but he stood shoulder-to-shoulder with baseball's Bill Veeck and the Browns' Mickey McBride on the honors platform.

It was generally acknowledged that the upward surge in the fortunes of professional sports in Cleveland had been led by Sutphin a decade earlier. His courageous sponsorship of a new Arena in 1937 seemed to have given life to the other branches of athletics and certainly stirred the fans into a rousing state of enthusiasm and civic pride that had not been seen since the winning days of the 1920 Indians.

In putting together a winning hockey team, Sutphin took much of the curse off its minor league status by running it along the same independent lines followed by the major league teams. Instead of being merely the temporary training ground for up-and-coming players bound for the big time, the Barons owned their own player's contracts, and while they had working arrangements with some of the NHL clubs, the Cleveland players were not jerked up and down from the minors to the majors in the usual yo-yo practice. The combination of players on the ice game after game was stable and steady, known and appreciated by the fans as a familiar lineup of Cleveland regulars.

Sutphin's hockey team was so good that the Barons overpowered the American Hockey League from 1937 on, leading some sports writers to describe them as "The New York Yankees of minor league hockey."

Al's best move was to reach into the ranks of the New York Rangers and to pluck out the legendary Bill Cook to be coach of his Cleveland team. Cook's great playing days were behind him, but the aura of great-

Sutphin, Veeck & McBride: Champions of 1948

ness followed him to the Barons and gave the team an extra dollop of glamour by association. Cook also turned out to be an outstanding coach. In another smart move, Sutphin later hired Bill Cook's brother, Bun, as the new manager of the Barons, while promoting Bill Cook to general manager. Too many Cooks did not spoil the broth. They made the Cleveland team better than ever.

When sports experts and fans try to determine which of the many Barons teams was the best, the arguments are inevitable. Many were outstanding. But the consensus probably would nominate the Barons of 1947-48 as the best of all. It was this club that racked up the most sensational record in the history of minor league hockey by winning 30 games in succession, skating off with the league championship and the Calder Cup. Eddie Coen, who served as publicity director of the Barons in the years 1946-1960, had a touch of awe in his voice as he remembered that season.

"People said then that if the Barons had been in the National Hockey League, they had a chance to make the playoffs," said Coen.

Among the outstanding Barons players were Johnny Holota, Fred

Thurier, Bobby Carse, Johnny Bower, Pete Leswick, Danny Sprout, Ab DeMarco and Bob Solinger.

"The Barons were the number one team in all of minor league hockey then," said Coen. "A lot of those years we'd have the championship locked up by Christmas."

But 1947-48 was the peak, and, quite in keeping with his charac-

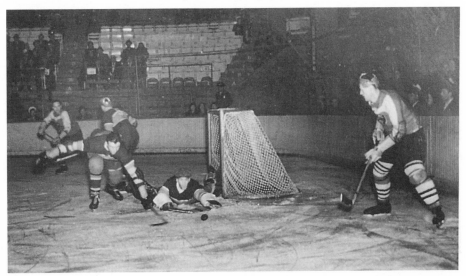

'48 Barons in action

ter, it was at that point that Al Sutphin reached the decision to withdraw from the sport and the great arena that had been the focal point of his life for nearly two decades. Always the competitor, he wanted to go out at the top, and he instinctively guessed that the moment had arrived.

The Champ was 55 years old in 1948 and he had carried a heavy burden since he was a teenager. A certain weariness had set in at last. The Arena and the finances required for its building had been a major burden in itself, but what made it an even more oppressive was that he had persuaded all of his friends to invest in the project.

Friendship ran deep with Al Sutphin. To the end of his life, he kept alive his relationships with former schoolmates, the men who had served with him in the army, his associates at Braden-Sutphin and many others he had met along the way. He regarded his promise to them as a sacred covenant.

It was a recession within a depression when the Arena opened its doors, and there can be no doubt that the success of that venture in those dark times was a direct result of Sutphin's salesmanship, determination and ingenuity. He kept the building busy around the clock and around the calendar, making it so profitable that at the end of 10 years he was in a position to sell it and pay back all of the original investors three times as much as they had risked on the venture. That was what he did in 1948's year of glory, making it, for him, a personal year of triumph, vindication and release. There was sadness at the parting of the ways, too, but the Champ was too busy reorganizing his life to let it show through.

Cleveland Plain Dealer (April 26, 1949)

The sale was a clean break with the past. On April 25th, 1949, Sutphin sold to three prominent Minneapolis businessmen. The price was two million dollars. The purchasers, part of a syndicate of Detroit interests, bought the Arena, the hockey team and its franchise, the building that housed the Braden-Sutphin Ink Company and all the real estate from Euclid to Chester. Sutphin even included his personal interest in the *Ice Capades.* It was as if the Champ was determined to wipe the slate clean. He didn't want any lingering ties tugging at his conscience. As all who knew him well were fully aware, Al Sutphin was incapable of taking a subordinate position. There could be no halfway measures. With him, it had to be all or nothing at all. He had chosen the latter.

Shortly before the sale, the Champ had figured that he had spent 260 nights on the road in the previous year. Even his vacations were frantic interludes. During one five-week stay in Florida, his secretaries sent out 40 telegrams, 1,000 pieces of mail, and spent $400 on long distance calls.

It was apparent by 1949 that Al would soon burn himself out in the interest of his business ventures, or he would have to unload a least some of his responsibilities so that he could approach a more normal way of life, one that would permit him to turn to the family that he loved so much.

What he had been missing at home suddenly occurred to the Champ one night. He confided as much to Howard Preston of the *Cleveland News* at the time of the Arena sale.

Preston had noticed that Sutphin appeared uncharacteristically glum during a hockey game. When he prodded Sutphin on the point, Al made the confidential disclosure that he had had a shock a few hours earlier.

"'Before I left home,' he told Preston, 'one of my daughters came downstairs in an evening gown. She was going to a formal dinner dance, and I hardly recognized her. It seemed to me, last I saw her, she was a little girl going to grammar school. I never saw her grow up.'

"Then and there," wrote Preston, "Sutphin began to make plans for getting out of the Arena. He has two boys, James, 13, and Albert Carlton, 9, and he made a vow they wouldn't suddenly appear before him as young men."

Sutphin had toyed with the idea of selling his hockey and Arena interests earlier, but the plan was not feasible (in his mind) until he had taken care of the hundreds of small stockholders, including so many personal friends. When that had been satisfactorily accomplished, the way was clear for a grand exit.

Looking back, the hockey entrepreneur said he would never again go through the "toil, sweat and tears" that it took to make the Arena a successful enterprise. He himself said the Arena succeeded through "fear."

"I was scared to death," he told friends. "I was afraid it would fail and I would be responsible. It was built with money given me by people, lots of little people, who trusted me. I couldn't let them down. But it's the worst feeling in the world to be gambling, if you want to put it that way, with other people's money. I'd never do it again."

Special recognition of his decision to withdraw from the Cleveland sports scene was given by Sutphin's old friend, Whitey Lewis of the *Press*.

"My Friend with the fluorescent four-in-hand, Al Sutphin, is going back to an existence of ease with printers, stationers, binders, bowlers, golfers, kids and convertibles. After 17 years of riding on or into the waves of public life in his home city, Al has sold out. He dumped the Arena, dumped the Barons, dumped their headaches and their glory.

"Meet Al Sutphin, common citizen again, proprietor of a large and money-making ink manufacturing establishment.

"Yet the guy never can be a common citizen here.

"As he bows out as president of the Arena and as president of the Barons of the American Hockey League in favor of an entirely new regime identified in adjacent columns, Sutphin leaves a neonized mark that should never be topped.

"For more than any other individual, more than any promoters who followed him, Sutphin quickened the pulse of Cleveland sports....

"One thing he'll never take away, and that's his imprint on sports here. He has been the strongest of all impelling forces in this field. He sprung open the gates and bade the people enter. They did, at good prices, for good entertainment in hockey and other fields, for enjoyment of an evening spent as spectators.

"To Al Sutphin I can say only that without you, my friend, everything would have been different. Brother, it might have been horrible.

"Thanks."

The Sutphin family welcomes home " The Happy Wanderer "

173 •

Overleaf: The Ice Man Goeth...

The Ice Man Goeth . . . .

YA SURE IT'S ON TH' LEGIT?

AL WAS FORMER C[...] OF CLEVELAND BOXI[...]

...FORMED AND W[...] OWNER OF THE ICE CAPADE[...]

ONE MAN MORE THAN OTHERS RESPONSIBLE FOR CLEVELAND'S SENSATIONAL RISE TO THE TOP OF THE SPORTS HEAP, AL SUTPHIN WHO, YESTERDAY, SOLD THE ARENA AND THE BARONS, PROVED SPORTS COULD BE SOLD TO THE PUBLIC TO DRAW HUGE CROWDS THEY'LL MISS

CHAPTER SIXTEEN

LIFE WITH FATHER

When Al Sutphin sold his beloved Arena and his championship Barons in the spring of 1949, a writer for the Cleveland News shrugged in disbelief at the Champ's announcement and scoffed at his declaration that from that time on he was going to "take it easy."

"Al Sutphin is neither dead nor Florence Nightingale," pointed out Ed McAuley, "so this department feels no disposition to pull out all the stops and beat the typewriter keys in slow and drippy accompaniment to something from Wagner at his saddest.

"We'll be seeing a lot of Al....He'll be beating our ears with the same old stories and blowing the same old, asphyxiating cigar smoke into our defenseless faces. He may be in line for a short salute, but certainly not for an epitaph...

"The guy is a dynamo, and unless long-suffering Mary Sutphin cracks down as firmly as she has been threatening to do for years, she'll find that the old boy simply has transferred his energy from one channel to another.

"I hope that one of the Sutphin kids grows up to be a writer," said McAuley's piece, "and sets down his or her memoirs in book form. The story would make *Cheaper by the Dozen* sound like the drabbest of family chronicles. It even would give *You Can't Take It With You* a good contest in the department of zany incidents."

Apocryphal stories do tend to accumulate around the name of prominent individuals. What may have set Al Sutphin apart was that most of the stories told about him were true. Many of the Sutphin stories stemmed from the single-mindedness that seized him when he was deeply involved in one of his major projects or when he was in such hot

Little Jane Sutphin

pursuit of an important Braden-Sutphin sales prospect that he seemed to exist in his own private compartment.

The Champ's characteristic devotion to business was not without effect on the personal side, but whenever he could, he tried to combine the two existences as he did one time in the late 1930's when he had to make a sales trip to Akron. He took his little daughter Jane with him on the trip for company.

The purpose of the Akron mission was to sell a rubber company on his idea of building the entrance of the proposed Arena in the shape of a giant tire.

The idea called for a very hard sell and an intense concentration of effort on the part of the salesman, i.e., Al Sutphin.

When Sutphin returned home from the trip to Akron, it was past midnight and the family was in bed. He thoughtfully tiptoed through the house to the master bedroom, where Mary's voice greeted him out of the darkness.

"Where's Jane?" she asked.

The question staggered the man of the house. So absorbed had he become in his mission, he had completely forgotten that little Jane was his traveling companion. Before he could sink into total panic, Mary took pity on him.

"It's all right," she said. "Jane is staying with Lil and Nettie (her aunts) in Akron. Where you left her!"

As Jane remembers that episode, she had been chosen to accompany her father to Akron because he loved to have one of his children along when he went on a long drive.

"He left me with mother's aunts at their music store in Akron that afternoon, and he was supposed to pick me up for the return trip to Cleveland before the store closed at 6 p.m."

When her father had failed to show up by 7:30, the puzzled aunts took Jane home with them. When no Al Sutphin had appeared by 10, Lil and Nettie proceeded on the reasonable assumption that the child would be their overnight guest.

"They cut the sleeves from one of their blouses and sewed them on one of their own small nighties, so my arms wouldn't get cold, and they put me to bed," Jane recalls. "I was only five years old. It was a lot of fun!"

But if there was fun on the Akron end of the Sutphin axis, there was utter dismay in Cleveland as the Champ was apprised of his over-

Cal Sutphin

sight. It was an incident destined to live forever in the Sutphin family annals. Al was never allowed to forget the time he had forgotten his own daughter.

In spite of his occasional oversights, the Champ believed himself to be a very stern father, and sometimes he was.

Young Cal got a taste of his father's firmness at an early age.

"It was around 1941 or 1942," he said. "I just recall being really little. I needed a haircut. Mother took me into Fort Myers and I threw a fit and the barber could not cut my hair.

"Mother took me back to the Farm and told Dad what had transpired. Immediately—and I mean immediately—Dad put me back in the car, took me back to the barber shop, didn't even get out of the car, just gave me the money for the haircut and sent me in. And I got a haircut without saying a word.

"Would you call that being intimidated or being obedient?"

Among the many recollections of Sutphin the Father that stand out in the memories of his family, there is unanimity on at least one point: "Dad was one guy you never lied to," said Mary Elizabeth.

Ernie Sutphen

Sutphin's Book of Family Rules and Regulations drew more than its share of grumbles and pleas for revision, but the Champ was always firm in his stand.

Al, on the other hand, was surprisingly understanding when it came to report cards and grades generally, perhaps because of his own high school experience. The only marks he really cared about on his children's cards were the ones given for Conduct and Effort — areas in which the Sutphin children always received high marks anyway. The Champ, in a real sense, was his own schoolmaster.

"Dad was an omnivorous reader," Alberta pointed out, "especially of historical novels and travel literature. And he made us all learn the names of the states and the capitals of the states at an early age. We often had dinner table examinations on that subject and similar subjects."

The image of the heavy-handed father was one Al didn't like for himself.

"If you think I'm difficult," he once told the kids, "you should have grown up with your grandfather. There was the original tough Dutchman!"

It isn't likely that the Champ was overstating the case when he described his father as a "tough Dutchman," but it was really an expression of his love and admiration.

Carleton Ernest Sutphen really was tough in the best sense of the word, one who had weathered all that life chose to offer without complaint or braggadocio. He didn't even protest when his family and friends decided to call him "Ernie."

His early life in the Middletown area, where he was born, had not been easy. He quit school in the 5th grade to help his family, going to work for the Sorg Paper Company and, once committed, stayed in the paper business for the rest of his working days. It was a successful career, one that took him to Ypsilanti, Michigan, where he became a division superintendent for the Peninsular Paper Company. He left that job in 1899 to move to Cleveland, where for 20 years he was a salesman for the Kingsley Paper Company. At the time of his retirement, he had been

Al with his parents, Ernie & Bess

associated with the Central Ohio Paper Company for 31 years and was one of the most highly respected men in the business to which he had contributed 63 years of his life.

Robert Seltzer of the *Cleveland Press* described him as "tall, sturdy, white-haired ... a man of considerable charm and courtliness."

Grandfather Sutphen never appered gruff to the six Sutphin grandchildren who found delight in his presence and affectionately called him "Gaga". None of their friends had a grandfather who could charm the birds out of the treetops with his mating whistles.

Part of Ernie's charm was his modest withdrawal into the shadows when the public spotlight focused on his son. No scene-stealer, he found all the satisfaction he needed in his son's success, and became more a companion to Al than a father as the two of them advanced in years.

The story is told about the time that Al and Ernie had dinner together in a restaurant at a time when Al had begun to use a cane because his hip gave him so much trouble. As the two of them were leaving the place, a waiter ran after them, holding the cane aloft.

"Hey," he said to Al, "your brother forgot his cane!"

"He's not my brother," grumbled Al, "he's my father! And the cane belongs to me!"

The "tough Dutchman" was father and confidante to Al, grandfather to his children, great-grandfather to another generation of descendants and friend to countless others. He lived to the age of 93.

Among Al's strict family rules was one relating to the daily newspapers. They were not, he emphasized, to be strewn about the house, lost in domestic by-play, or removed from his ready reach. He expected the newspapers to be neatly folded on his bed at night, ready for the reading. If they were not, he would pad into the children's bedrooms and order them out from under the covers for a mandatory house search.

"After that," said son Jimmy, "you didn't forget to put the newspapers on his bed!"

But more than the newspapers had to be at Al's fingertips when he took to his bed for the night. It was almost a ceremonial moment when, in total relaxation, he could cater to all of his personal whims and weaknesses. On the bedside table there had to be a big pitcher of ice water and a large bowl of popcorn. And his favorite Ology cigars, to be sure. It was a nightcap combination that would have rendered a lesser man unconscious.

"How he was able to read in bed, eat popcorn, drink ice water, and smoke cigars all at once," marveled son Jim, "I don't know. I mean, I just don't know how he did it."

The last thing he did before going to sleep was to read the two afternoon newspapers that were published in Cleveland at that time, the *News* and the *Press*. And when he awoke the next morning, he had to have the *Plain Dealer*.

"Dad's romance with the newspapers continued all his life," said daughter Alberta, "and he arranged it so that the newspapers from Cleveland followed him all through his European travels. At home, his reading of the morning *Plain Dealer*, set on a silver stand on the breakfast table, was a morning ritual."

Those pungent cigars were not just a bedtime weakness. The Champ walked around during his waking hours in his own personal cloud of smoke. When he wasn't smoking one of his cigars, he usually had a lighted pipe in his mouth. The pipe, in fact, was his weapon of choice, and it was so closely identified with him that his stationery bore his likeness in silhouetted profile, pipe in mouth.

He had other habits, appetites and customs that set him apart from most people. Because he liked the cold, and perhaps because he himself was the principal air polluter in the family, Al insisted that the air conditioning system of the family car be kept in operation at all times, summer and winter. It didn't strike him as odd that other motorists had their heaters going in the winter.

Al's girls perform in Sutphin's Little Theater (inset: Little Theater mark)

But Al liked cold weather even to the extent of sleeping in the screened porch of the house on Berkshire Road in the middle of January, on nights when the mercury had dropped far below the freezing mark. Mary Sutphin, who never ceased to marvel over her husband's eccentricity in the matter, usually placed a canvas over the blanket covering Al's recumbent form during the night so the snow coming through the screening would not soak him as it melted.

It follows that the Champ's love of a cold environment led him to keep his office temperature as low as possible. Jane McManamon had to shiver through many a session of letter dictation when her pen was ready to fall from her benumbed fingers. Mary Sutphin fought back at home against the low-temperature syndrome by following Al around the house, upping the thermostatic reading as fast as he lowered it.

Mary also had to cope with her husband's strange ways at the dinner table. He never ate lunch until 3 or 4 in the afternoon. He simply didn't believe in eating any earlier in the day. And when he did eat, it was along lines calculated to make the most hardened chef reel backward and grab for support. It was said, not lightly, that Al Sutphin had a cast-iron stomach, and there were times, indeed, when it would not have surprised anybody if he had ordered a cast-iron sandwich. He was especially fond of Chinese food. And whatever the entree might be, his favorite dessert was a pineapple soda with double scoops of strawberry ice cream.

In any family reunion, the recollections of the past invariably center on the Champ's likes and dislikes, and all the home front episodes that so often grew out of the routines followed by the Head of the Family.

The Champ loved to play cards and his favorite game was gin rummy, but when he played cards with the children, he usually elected the game of Little Casino because he thought it to be educational as well as entertaining in the way it taught mathematics to the kids.

Al took special pride in showing off his quartet of little girls.

"My memories include going to Case-Western Reserve football games at Case Tech's Van Horn Field at the foot of Cedar Hill," said Jane. "We wore matching wool maroon jump suits with matching aviator helmets with chin straps. Dad marched us behind him, single file, through the stands with everyone nudging one another at the sight of us, I loved it! Dad always knew how to get the crowd's attention," said Jane.

One of the most memorable nights in the family's history took place in 1937, the opening of the new Arena, but the historic occasion was remembered by the girls for something other than the premiere doings of their father's creation on Euclid Avenue.

"Mary remembers opening night of the Arena because she wore her first formal," said Jane. "I was so jealous. She was 13, a young lady. I was a baby of 11, but had dreams of being 25.

"And I remember what happened when they introduced my mother to the assembled crowd. She stood in a bright spotlight and the star of the Ice Follies, Roy Shipstad, presented her with a dozen American Beauty roses.

The spotlight went down and the announcer's voice introduced my grandmother Sutphen, and, in the dark, the roses were snatched from my mother and presented to my grandmother: The same bouquet was snatched in the dark for a dozen ladies, all the directors' wives, with no one in the crowd ever knowing!"

The opening of the Arena took place during the Depression, she pointed out. "Only one bouquet to an opening in those days!"

The hiring of Bill Cook as the coach of the Barons in 1937 not only affected the destiny of the hockey team, it brought about a new chapter in the lives of the Sutphin family. Through Bill Cook and his brothers, Fred and Alex, the Sutphins discovered the vacation delights of Canada; specifically the area around Kingston, in Ontario Province.

The Guest Cottage

The Sutphin Cottage

Cook owned a couple of cottages on the St. Lawrence River, near Kingston, which he rented out to the Sutphins every summer for about 12 years.

"Dad leased the two homes that were quite rustic, Victorian type, on several acres of land right on the river," Alberta Sutphin Stoney remembers.

"We'd go to Kingston every year between 1941 and 1952 and we would stay there through the summer, from June until September. Dad saw to it that it wasn't all play. We all worked at Kingston in one capacity or another. The first few years, I recall, my sister Mary drove the speedboat and took family and guests fishing. Jane and I helped Mother. Brother Jim cleaned the fish, dozens of them, every night.

"Dad always believed in all of us being very much involved in representing Braden-Sutphin and entertaining our guests."

The dozen years or so that the family spent in Kingston were treasured and generated a lot of happy memories as well as recollections of odd happenings. One of these involved an old Ford convertible that the Sutphin sisters drove into town one time to see a motion picture. Upon their return, they parked the car at the top of a hill next to a cottage.

"Whoever the driver was," said Jim Sutphin, "she forgot to employ the emergency brake and in no time at all the car began to roll downhill, through the trees, and toward the St. Lawrence River!

"My dad and Bill Cook and some of the others were sitting there and they saw the car drifting by, not knowing that there was nobody behind the wheel ..."

Jim Sutphin

The downward course of the car did catch everybody's attention, however, because it was headed for the river. Alarmed, the men jumped up and ran after it.

"They slid down the embankment and into the river," continued Jim, " and it was a miracle that they didn't hurt themselves. At any rate, when they got to the scene, the car had plunged into the water and had turned upside down. They swam around it, frantically opening doors, but there was nobody in the car.

"The incident certainly caused great commotion, though. When my sisters came down from the second floor room and asked what was going on, the fathers, dripping wet, weren't too pleased. Not at all."

But if young Jim Sutphin was merely a bystander when the car rolled down the hill, he was a principal figure in the incident that involved the family's outboard motor boat.

"I had been learning how to run the outboard, and practicing because my father insisted that I be capable of running the boat before I could go out by myself."

Feeling that he was ready to demonstrate his ability, Jim persuaded his father to get into the boat and go for a ride with him.

"I wrapped a rope around the starter ... and pulled at the rope, as you would do in those days. My dad was sitting in the middle of the boat, me in the back ..."

The rope wrapped itself around his father's head.

"Fortunately it didn't hurt him, but it did sting." admitted Jim.

Al Sutphin shook off the rope wrapped around his head like a turban, sighed, and said: "Well, I guess you need a little more practice."

It was during a summer stay at the Canadian cottage in 1950 that Jim

Sutphin, then 18, learned anew what a practical joker his father could be. Among the guests at that time was Aunt Margaret Moran, whose age he guessed at that time to be "somewhere near 60."

"Aunt Margaret and I were going to drive my father's Chrysler from Kingston back to Cleveland. This was a real car, with wooden sides. Slick. Our plan was to get up really early, about 5 o'clock in the morning, and drive the 480 miles to Cleveland in one day. In those days, of course, there were no expressways, just Highway 2 to Buffalo, and then Route 20 to Cleveland.

Aunt Margaret

"Normally, leaving so early, we would say our goodbyes the night before the trip. Hardly anybody ever got up to say goodbye, but this particular morning we were surprised to find everybody out of bed and on hand to see us off. We thought that was a bit unusual, but pretty nice.

"It took about 45 minutes to the Customs Station, and there we noticed the people in the booth were looking out at us and laughing. As we drove on, though, a number of people in the cars that passed us would honk and wave. It was pretty amazing, and we wondered why people were being so friendly. We found out, finally, when we stopped to buy gas. When I walked around the car to get to the gas tank, I saw a big sign that has been fastened on the rear trunk. It said, 'Just Married.'"

"Aunt Margaret and I got a big kick out of that, wondering what other people thought as they passed the car with an 18-year-old and a woman about 40 years older. We realized then why everybody at the cottage got up bright and early to say goodbye to us."

The Sutphin sense of humor. It never quit.

Overleaf: Al at his first love, The Braden-Sutphin Ink Company

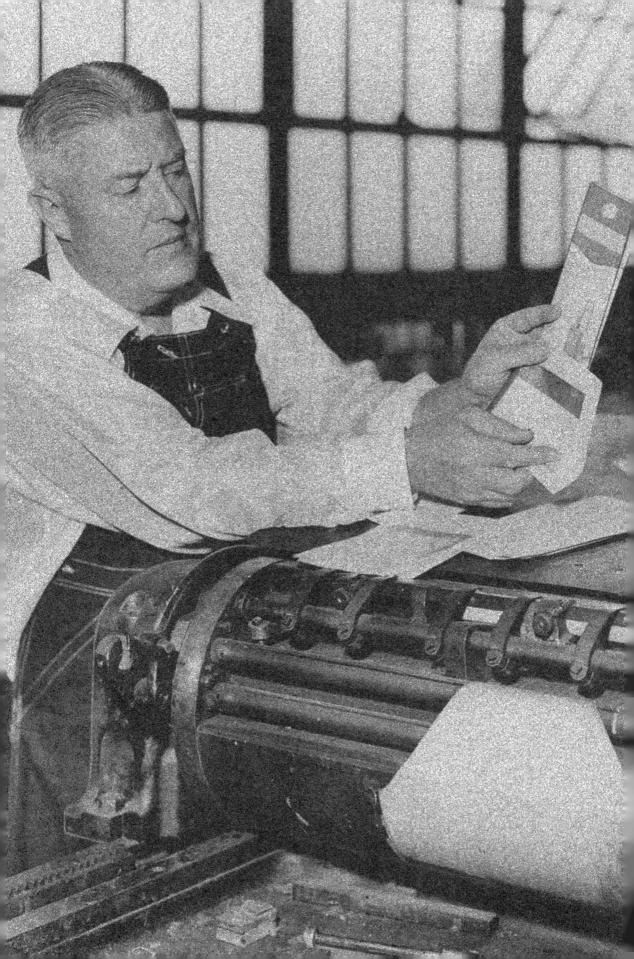

CHAPTER SEVENTEEN

NEW DIRECTIONS

Less than a year after he sold the Arena and the hockey team, announcing his determination to devote more of his time and attention to his family and private interests, the Champ accepted an appointment as chairman of the Board of Athletics of John Carroll University.

The announcement in November, 1949, took all the Sutphin-watchers by surprise. In that collegiate post, Al obviously would be called upon to make full use of his promotional genius to propel John Carroll into the ranks of major college sports. His specific responsibility would be to elevate Carroll's basketball program into the big time.

This new undertaking was hardly to be expected of a man who was moving toward a life of retirement ease next to the hearth side. Observers of the local scene were convinced that Sutphin simply was going from the Arena frying pan into the collegiate fire. He never before had to operate within the strict boundaries of college competition, for one thing, and never had to work as part of a committee under a university administration. There were bound to be irksome restrictions, including consultations with higher powers. It would be a novel experience. He always had been his own man, with full control of his own projects.

When he accepted the John Carroll post, Sutphin explained that he just couldn't stay on the sidelines entirely.

"I want to see Carroll achieve national prominence," he said. "I've had enough of hard work. Now I want to have fun, and I think I can do it with Carroll."

He revealed at the same time that only six weeks earlier he had turned down an opportunity to become president of the Cleveland Indians. A local group which had raised money to buy the team had told him that they would go ahead with the transaction if he would head the club.

That collateral piece of news probably was of more interest to Cleveland sports fans than the disclosure that he was accepting the post of John Carroll athletic board chairman. It had been rumored for a long

Tris Speaker

time that Sutphin one day would take over the Indians, and there was the optimistic feeling among Indian fans that he would give them the kind of success that he had given to the city's hockey followers. His rejection of the opportunity to run the baseball team was more surprising to those who knew him well than his acceptance of the university job. He enjoyed all sports, but his lifetime love was baseball.

Sutphin had been a rooter for the Cleveland Indians since childhood and he had bought season tickets to their games from his earliest working years. Sutphin loved to talk about the baseball stars he had met, and one of his favorites stories had to do with Hall-of-Famer Tris Speaker.

Although a celebrated all-time all-star, Tris Speaker also was a perfectionist, never satisfied with his own performance. Once, in mid-season, Speaker wanted some extra practice to sharpen his batting techniques. To do that, he needed several young players to shag flies, field his grounders, and feed him the ball. He asked young Al Sutphin to round up a few buddies to help him out in exchange for a few dollars in pay.

Sutphin and his friends obliged the great Speaker, thoroughly enjoying their brush with the baseball immortal. When he talked about Speaker, he also liked to tell a story that underlined the fine human side of the famous player-manager who led the Indians to their first American League pennant and World Series victory over Brooklyn in 1920.

Long after Speaker had retired from an active role with the Indians, he was named chairman of a special program to honor another former Indians player and long-time play-by-play radio announcer, Jack Graney. The plan was to call Graney out to the pitcher's mound at League Park before a regular game and there to receive a special award from Speaker.

Before the game, Sutphin had met with Speaker and his wife in a restaurant, and he noticed that the famous "Gray Ghost" was uncommonly quiet during the dinner meal. That didn't strike him as unusual. He assumed that Speaker was preoccupied with the preparation of remarks for the evening's program.

After Tris had excused himself—he had to be at the ball park early to attend to program details—Mrs. Speaker confided to Sutphin that the reason her husband was so low in spirit was that he had hoped to announce a cash gift of $10,000 to his old friend Graney as the surprise of the night's affair. But his fund-raising drive had fallen short by $1,000.

Jack Graney

Sutphin rushed to the ball park and proposed to Speaker that the two of them underwrite the amount needed. Speaker delightedly wrote out a check for $500 and Sutphin matched the amount. Graney got his $10,000.

At John Carroll University, Sutphin's principal responsibility as head of the athletic board was to promote Carroll's basketball program by getting its team into the big time of collegiate play. His only previous experience with basketball was the professional team he had owned briefly, the Cleveland Rebels. It had not been a happy adventure. Nevertheless, he spoke optimistically of his plans to upgrade the John Carroll team.

"The day will come, perhaps in the next few years," he predicted, "When Carroll basketball teams will carry the school's colors into Boston Gardens and Madison Square Garden."

Disillusionment with that ambitious program set in early. By September of 1950, less than 10 months after he had taken on the Carroll assignment, the Champ turned in his resignation. He cited the demands on his time, the wish to see more of his family, and the desire to withdraw from the active sports scene in all capacities except spectator.

In the same statement he sought to quash rumors of friction in his relationship with the university.

"There have been rumors that affairs between John Carroll and myself have not been harmonious," he said, "Nothing is further from the truth. My association with the university has been most pleasant."

It was, all things considered, a strange episode in the career of this energetic sports promoter. It probably was a simple mistake in judgment. Al Sutphin had always been his own man in whatever he did. He lived and worked throughout his career as the man who held the reins. In the university system, he was one of many—the chairman of the committee but not the boss. And perhaps there was an inner embarrassment at finding himself in the high academic world without even a high school diploma. Whatever the reasons, he was uncomfortable in his post at John Carroll.

"Without extreme effort," he wrote in his letter of resignation to Fr. Welfle, president of the university, "it is very difficult to be successful, and I would not want a half-hearted effort on my conscience. I assure you that I will always be grateful for the fine honor bestowed upon me by the university."

It is worth noting that, unknown to others, Al was having concerns over his own health. The hip that he had injured was plaguing him more as he grew older, he was having weight problems, and there were too many days and nights when he simply did not feel well. He underwent hospitalization for tests at the end of 1951 and was given a discouraging prognosis. The doctors told him he was suffering from diabetes and that his hip ailment was beyond correction. He was also cautioned, for his own good to "walk as little as possible."

Their words were as feathers in the wind.

Al Sutphin had set his own pace of living from childhood days, and it was of a tempo meant to take him everywhere as fast as possible, enable him to see everything worth seeing, and keep him an active player on the field of life as long as possible.

Instead of putting on the brakes, he regarded the time to be more appropriate for a step-up in his pace of living.

Shortly after he had been given the "slow down" signal by the doctors, the Champ traveled to the Olympic Games in Helsinki, taking along his two sons, and later meeting up with wife Mary in Rome. One afternoon in that city, as Sutphin tells it:

"While Mary and I were casually strolling through the park, we met Bob Hope and his attorney from Cleveland, and Bob's new lady singer (not Dorothy Lamour). Know Bob personally inasmuch as we, on a number of occasions, split better than $20,000 on a fifty-fifty basis during his Cleveland engagements in the Cleveland Arena. Therefore paused to chat.

"Bob expressed surprise that I was still wearing the red tie and explained that Larry Atkins (fight promoter) and Whitey Lewis (sports editor of the Cleveland Press) had always assured him that my wearing of the red tie was a promotional racket. And that I was still wearing the red cravat 4,000 miles from home was really surprising to him.

"While we were chatting, our Cal came along and I asked Cal if he knew who Bob was. And Cal instantly answered in the affirmative. 'Bob Hope,' and I was pleased that he knew.

Bing Crosby & Bob Hope

"Right after this, our Jimmy came along (I left him to the mercy of a dilatory waiter to pay the bill) and I asked Jimmy the same question. Jimmy instantly replied, 'Oh, sure. Bing Crosby.'

"With that, Bob grabbed Jimmy around the neck, drew him to him affectionately and remarked: 'There is always one fresh son in every family!'

"Personally, I did not exactly enjoy Jimmy's witticism, but I did get a thrill out of Hope's reaction. Perhaps Jimmy learned not to be a wisecracker in the presence of America's greatest wit."

Cal also was highly amused by the interchange between his brother and Bob Hope on that day in Rome long ago.

"I will never forget that Hope loved Jim's response and literally grabbed him and gave him a Dutch rub on the head," he said.

There was an entertaining sequel to this encounter in Rome some 8 years later, in 1960, at the time of the summer Olympics. On a stroll this time the Sutphins met Bing Crosby and his wife, Kathy. Al recalled, for the enjoyment of the Crosbys, the encounter with Bob Hope in 1952 in the same city and of the intentional misidentification of Crosby's old film partner by young Jimmy.

Bing, highly amused by the story, put a playful headlock on Jim by way of punishment for confusing him with Bob Hope.

A year after being sternly advised by the doctors to slow down, Al and Mary took their three-month journey around the world with a daily schedule that would have exhausted a fourteen-year-old. They were both

This is Your Life, Al Sutphin

so excited over their upcoming cruise that they walked into a trap set for them by their children and close friends in August of 1959. It was supposed to be merely a nice anniversary dinner, but it turned out to be a celebration of their long marriage along the lines of the television program, *This is Your Life.*

It was a highly sentimental experience, of course; so much so that Al wrapped up his reactions in a letter addressed To The Sutphin Family, dated August 24, 1959:

"Dearest All,

"Little did I think as your Mother and I left the Alcazar last Saturday night to go to Mary Elizabeth's house for our Anniversary Dinner that I was walking into perhaps the most memorable night of my life.

"Have tuned in on television to the program, *This Is Your Life*, many times and always thought it a most interesting program and always considered that it must be a great thrill to the person featured...

"None of you will ever have any idea just exactly the emotion stirred within me by your wonderful presentation of 'Old Friends'.

"First, may I advise that it was a complete, 100% surprise.

"And when Bob Leitch started reading me the inaugural thinking of *This Is Your Life*, even then I did not comprehend what was to follow ...

Some "Old Friends", l. to r., Mary, Mrs. Dick Kroesen, Al, Mr. & Mrs. Tom Manning

"First Bob introduced my father whom I have known rather intimately for 70 [?] years, and I thought nothing unusual about his being there.

"Next Albert Betz, 60 years, started in grammar school with Mooks and have been inseparable friends ever since....

"Norbert Stein, 28 years...my right hand in all Arena affairs...The introductions of Loretta Hoynes and Gertie McDonnell, 40 years, gave me a thousand nostalgic memories...Margaret Moran, over 50 years....Perhaps Margaret won't like my mentioning the 50 years of our friendship!

"Then came Mame Leitch, better known as Hoppy, the lovely mother of Bob and Harry Leitch, the scalawags, and who would have a better right to attend?

"The Tom Mannings, over 30 years....Paul and Anne Hoynes, 45 years....

"All of these were a complete surprise. Incidentally, you all had a very clever way of introducing the guests, with the voice coming from the outer room and my being unable to see the possessor of that voice.

"Then came the Tobins, 26 years...the Danners, 40 years...the Estes', over 50 years...Came the voice of Don Rogers, 44 years...

"And then came the introduction that started the flow of tears, Gwen

The Browns & the Sutphins travel on the Queen Elizabeth following the 1959 football season

Russell, 40 years. The wife of one of my finest friends and one who made visits to Buffalo memorable events in my life...and Dorothy Carver, another 40 year friend...Lucille Garber Ford, nearly 40 years...Lucille came to our Wedding, and was the youngest person invited (eight months old!).

"What price friends!!!

"Came the voice of Jim Bedell, another 40 year friend and...

"The last guests introduced, although from Cleveland, knocked me for a loop. The Paul Browns.

"No one knows better than I do that Paul Brown never leaves his training camp once the Cleveland Browns enter their training at Hiram, and it would take a friendship of very high standing to get Paul to do so. The fact that he came to our Night of Nights will be a tribute that Mary and I will appreciate all our lives.

"You Kids know your Father so well and know that I am without question the greatest sentimentalist of your acquaintanceship now and in the days to come. Therefore, I will always regard last Saturday night as just about the finest night of my life and I thank you so much for your terrific effort.

"They tell me the dinner was wonderful. That I will never know. Eating was most difficult for me that night...

"Mary and I are indeed fortunate. No Mother or Father were ever graced with finer, more thoughtful, and considerate children than we.

"God Bless You All,

"Always yours,

"Champ"

While all of the many overseas journeys of the Sutphin family were memorable in one way or the other, the one that was undertaken in 1964 probably qualified as the most unusual—in one aspect, at least.

This may have been the only honeymoon in history that also was a group tour. The story is best told by Cal Sutphin, the groom.

"At Christmas in 1963, I was engaged to be married the following September, 1964. But Dad called and made me an offer that I couldn't refuse. He asked us to move our wedding up to July 11, 1964. If we did, our honeymoon could be a trip to Europe with four sisters, three brothers-in-law, my brother, Jim, and 'a few additional friends', or seventeen others.

Cal & Sandy Sutphin

"Even if it did not sound like a good idea, when Dad had an idea it was almost always a good one," Cal conceded. He and his fiancee thought over the proposition and found it acceptable.

"We got married Saturday, July 11, 1964. Sandy and I spent Saturday, Sunday and Monday on our own, then, on Tuesday, joined the family at the Abbey Hotel in New York.

. "Wednesday, July 15, we sailed on the *Queen Elizabeth*, landed in Cherbourg, France, on July 20, toured some of Dad's World War I battle sites, spent significant time in France and Spain, and also saw parts of Austria and Switzerland. We sailed home from Cherbourg on August 20th.

"As well as being a rather unusual honeymoon, it was very special, and we have lots of wonderful memories of that trip. "One of the funniest circumstances occurred right at the outset of our trip. When Sandy and I reached our stateroom we discovered there were no beds. Champ had instructed the Queen's crew to remove them! So how could you forget honeymooning with my father and sixteen other members of our family?"

The Champ reserved a bus for the family's three weeks of travel, and was in top form as a touring guide touring. Whenever a sight came in view that he especially wanted everyone to admire, he would yell loudly: "Panorama, Everyone!" The yell took its place as one of those standing jokes in family get-togethers in later years.

This kind of chronological recital deals only with highlight movements of a man constantly in motion. The doctors who told Al Sutphin to "walk as little as possible" were well-intentioned, but everyone who knew the man rejected the advice as realistically unrealistic.

Columnist Ed McAuley was one of these when he wrote in the *Cleveland News* in 1954:

"Sutphin tried everything from public skating to six-day bike races in a 12-year career in which he set a man-killing pace which his assistants

On the "Panorama" Tour

often found too fast. (Now) Grandpa Al at 59 has reached the point at which it is possible for a half-dozen ordinary men at least to keep track of his movements. No number could keep up with him."

"He's off to Europe for the Olympics and an air tour of the continent. He's in New York for the World Series. He's on his way to his winter home in Fort Myers, Florida, but by way of Baltimore. Or he's motoring through Mexico. He's taking a cold plunge in the lake at his place in Kingston, Ontario, or he's off to Boston to help a customer solve a knotty problem in the use of high-rate printing inks.

"All this, mind you, in the guise of semi-retirement..."

Apart from his continued preoccupation with overseas travel and the affairs of his ink company, Al turned more and more to thoughts about his Florida estate as a central concern. He was highly perturbed in 1960 when he learned that the county was planning a new bridge from Fort Myers to Cape Coral. It appeared from preliminary plans that the bridge supports would be placed next to his beloved Farm. In 1961, with this fear in mind, he bought an additional 125 feet of river frontage next to the Farm as a buffer if the bridge were built. He also led neighbors and homeowners in a determined campaign opposing the project, arguing against it in large newspaper ads and commercial time on television, pointing out that the bridge would change the character of the entire Caloosahatchie River area with its heavy traffic generating noise and noxious fumes.

Commodore Sutphin vs. The Cape Coral Bridge

Sutphin did some fuming of his own over the bridge and in 1969 threatened to sell his riverfront property in Fort Myers and take up life in another part of Florida.

He also went so far as to buy a 20 unit motel, the Gulf Manor Motel in Tarpon Springs, an acquisition that puzzled people close to him. The general assumption was that Al in this instance was firing a warning shot across the bow of the city and the county officials in Fort Myers. He had risen to high stature in that community over the years because of his active participation in civic affairs, local sports, charities, contributions, and his acknowledged hospitality. The local newspaper always kept a close eye on which celebrities were guests on the Farm at any given time and interviewed most of them. Such glamour necessarily rubbed off on Al himself.

The importance of the Champ, however, did not deter the county in its plans for the new bridge, nor did his motel purchase in Tarpon Springs.

But if the bureaucrats in Fort Myers were indifferent to Al's menacing move, the civic leaders in Tarpon Springs were instantly aware that a dynamic new force had become part of their community.

For his part, playing to a new audience seemed to fan the embers and bring forth some of the old time Sutphin fire. His usual public-spirited generosity was still operative and it naturally won him a lot of attention not normally given to newcomers.

Our Gulf Manor Motel taken from the Bayou at Tarpon Springs, Florida

The Gulf Manor at Tarpon Springs

It was Al Sutphin who voluntarily donated the fireworks for the city's pyrotechnic display over Whitcomb Bayou on the holiday. Mayor George Tsourakis described that celebration as 'the most successful Fourth of July in the history of our town." He also presented the Champ with the key to the city and a "Citizens Participation Certificate" for his "fine civic gesture." The daily newspaper ran a 3-column picture of Al and Mary receiving these honors from the mayor and the president of the Jaycees.

It was amazing how deeply the Champ had become involved in Tarpon Springs in the short time he owned the Gulf Manor Motel, especially considering that he was never more than a part-time resident. A 1967 letter addressed to "The Sutphin Family and to All Salesman" hints at his widespread involvement:

"The baseball team at Tarpon Springs got into the high school championship tournament which was played at Fort Myers, and we were able to offer the courtesy of the Big House to the baseball team, their coaches, and some high school officials, and they were delighted indeed.

"They thanked us so profusely and so did the Tarpon Springs newspaper, of which we are sending you a clipping."

An editorial in the newspaper read in part as follows:

"Tarpon Springs High baseball fans own a debt of gratitude to Al Sutphin, owner of the Gulf Manor Motel and a part-time resident here. The boy's parents and teachers will be interested to know that Mr. Sutphin was highly impressed with the team, both on and off the field."

Tarpon Springs Welcomes the Sutphins

For all the laudatory attention given him in Tarpon Springs, there never was any doubt that the Champ's heart still was firmly attached to the Farm in Fort Myers. He had gotten too old and his infirmities were growing too severe for him to start up all over again in some other area. He had become a year-around resident of Florida and Fort Myers was home, bridge or no bridge.

If there had been a milepost along the Sutphin way to mark the date of his retirement, it would have been that same year, 1967, when Al suffered a frightening blackout while on a train to New York City. To make the trip even worse, the train had three accidents on the run east. That brush with the Great Beyond did more to slow the Champ than any of his doctor's warnings.

Al "holds court" yet again...The Cleveland Open (1963)

*Lou Groza & Otto Graham of the Cleveland Browns with Al
at the 1953 Ribs & Roast Dinner at the Cleveland Hotel*

Another night, NO fun!...Bob Leitch, Al, Harry Leitch & Jim Sutphin

Al's greatest gig, "Inky Jim's" bachelor party
174 speakers & 1 lonely guest (Sept. 6, 1958)

Overleaf: ...back at the Arena

MEANWHILE, BACK AT THE ARENA

In all his travels, no matter how distant, the Champ's mind never lost track of the Arena and the hockey team he had brought into being. His daily scanning of the newspapers from his home city—and mail copies followed him all over the globe—invariably began with an intensive reading of the sports pages. If it were not the hockey playing season, he could count on the entertainment pages to fill him in on the current attractions at the Arena.

There was a time not long after he had relinquished ownership that he found the news of his beloved creation on the front pages across the nation.

What had happened at the Arena was described by police as a riot. Others called it the world's first rock 'n' roll concert, officially billed as the Moon Dog Coronation Ball, the creation of a disc jockey Alan Freed. Freed's nightly show, began in 1950, had stressed music at first dubbed "rhythm and blues", and he called himself the "King of the Mondays."

The only advance notice of the show was a single paragraph in the *Plain Dealer* entertainment pages. It was noted that "Tiny Grimes' Band and a half-dozen recording blues-and-rhythm singers are being combined in a 'Moon Dog Coronation Ball' at the Arena tomorrow night."

The turnout on the night of March 21, 1952 was the largest crowd ever to attend a single event at the Arena. The *Cleveland Press* said that more than 25,000 people were on hand, intent on enjoying themselves no matter what it took. In the aftermath, nobody was sure just how many people actually made their way into the building. In the terminology of the day, the *Press* reported that "hepcats" jammed every inch of the big Arena floor.

This was the world's first rock concert, an explosive beginning to an explosive era in music. It was Woodstock under a roof. Peter Hastings, author and photographer, who was present to take pictures of the ball, told Jane Scott of the *Plain Dealer*: "I can still see that crowd below us...getting bigger all the time. It was frightening. I took the picture. Then we got out of there as fast as we could."

The Moondog Coronation Ball

William Lemmon of radio station WJW, was "absolutely flabbergasted" by the scene at the Arena that historic night.

"It was madness," he said. "I saw knives flashing. People without tickets broke down the doors. We were up in the press box and couldn't get out for three hours."

The entertainers on the bill included the well-known Dominoes and the likes of Paul Williams, Danny Cobb and Varetta Dillard, but what they had to offer became secondary to the riotous nature of the crowd in the seats, the aisles and the rafters. Even so, the rhythm-and-blues program that filtered through the mob scene was given rough treatment by the critic for the *Call and Post*, Cleveland's black newspaper.

Women's Editor Valena Minor Williams wrote:

"The shame of the situation lies not in the frustrated crowd that rushed the Arena, but in a community which allows a program like this to continue and to exploit the Negro teensters!"

The *Call and Post* summed up the program as: "Garbage, trash, a shocking display of gutbucket blues and lowdown rhythms."

On the other hand, Norm N. Nite, former disk jockey in Cleveland

and New York and an acknowledged expert on rock 'n' roll, saw the ball as an historic event.

"If rock had any particular beginning, it was on March 21, 1952," he told the *Plain Dealer*. "Freed played black music when no white man was playing it....Freed paved the way for Frankie Lyman and the TeenAgers, Little Richard and Chuck Berry to get exposure to white fans."

The Rock 'N' Roll Hall of Fame + Museum, inset: Alan Freed

Legendary radio veteran Bill Randle, a leading authority on popular music of all kinds, agrees with Nite's judgment.

"It was the beginning of the acceptance of black popular music as a force in radio. It was the first big show of its kind where the industry saw it as big business."

While the near-riot at the Arena was a terrifying experience for Freed, it propelled him into the front ranks of American disk jockeys and gave him lasting fame as the man who launched rock 'n' roll.

His career, though, trailed off into an unhappy ending when he was linked with payola scandals and another riotous rock 'n' roll show in Boston. He had been shuffled out of radio entirely by the time of his death at age 43 in 1965.

The irony is that, despite its tumultuous beginning in the Arena, rock 'n' roll music itself quickly gained public acceptance and Cleveland ultimately became the home of the Rock 'n' Roll Hall of Fame Museum on the downtown lakefront. Al Sutphin lived long enough to see the new music take shape, and whatever he may have thought of the art form itself, it undoubtedly pleased him that his splendid Arena racked up another historic first in the world of entertainment.

Many changes had taken place at the big sports facility in the five years since the building's ownership had been transferred to the syndicate of buyers. Richard Kroesen, owner of the Cleveland Sports Goods Company, was named to replace Bernard Ryan as Arena president in 1951.

Kroesen was a wartime buddy of Sutphin's, and, like the Champ, had been active in Cleveland sports circles during most of his life. Dick Kroesen was a popular choice to head the Arena, although he claimed to be puzzled by his selection.

"I guess they figured that since I lived through the whole thing with Sutphin, I must know a lot about it," he told reporters.

Kroesen's first announcement was that James Hendy would continue as general manager of the Arena and the Barons, and that all of the employees would be retained. It was the kind of announcement that Al Sutphin undoubtedly applauded. While he had left behind him a most efficient management, there wasn't any question but that the operation of the Arena had sagged in the intervening years.

The key executive, apart from the administrative president, was General Manager Jim Hendy, recognized as one of the most knowledgeable hockey experts in the country. Prior to assuming the Arena post in mid-summer of 1949, he had been president of the United States Hockey League. He had immediately formed a close partnership with Coach Fred Cook, and the Barons team that the Champ had brought together continued on its winning ways. Hendy, twice honored as the executive of the year in all of professional hockey, waged a desperate campaign to move the Barons into the National Hockey League in the late 1950's, but failed.

"He just couldn't raise enough money," said Eddie Coen, the team's publicity director and one of the Sutphin holdovers. "He spent untold hours on the telephone, but he just couldn't get it."

The hockey team's success was only part of the Arena story. The facility could not prosper on hockey alone. The Arena had to be an active entertainment center on the other 300-plus nights of the year.

What the new owners missed most sorely in their administration of the Arena was the showmanship and salesmanship of Al Sutphin himself. Nobody realized just how much he personally was responsible for the facility's success until his hand was no longer at the tiller. With his departure, the prosperity of the Arena began its decline. The downward course continued

Sugar Ray Robinson

through the 1950's, despite the desperate flailing of management. In 1962, John Lemmo was hired as general manager of the Arena and his initial survey of the situation was entirely depressing.

"I was hired on a one-year salvage job," he told Bob Dolgan of the *Plain Dealer* later. "The plan was either to try to build the Arena back up or try to sell it. The building was openly for sale for $1 million, but nobody could find a buyer!"

Lemmo, a capable administrator who later became director of operations for Cleveland Stadium, was unable to stem the red ink at the Arena despite an effort to bolster the program of attractions with such events as the roller derby, more wrestling shows and lengthening the runs of such strong draws as the *Ice Capades* and the *Ice Follies*. The Arena still lost money.

"It was almost impossible to make it pay," said Lemmo. "I had a trimmed down staff, only three people working for me, but it was a loser just about every year."

One of the Arena memories that most patrons recalled in its closing years had tragic overtones. It was a fight between Sugar Ray Robinson and Irish Jimmy Doyle in which Robinson's welterweight title was at stake. Doyle was knocked out. As he fell, his head appeared to hit the floor of the ring with unusual force. He died the next day.

Robinson was one of the principals in another Arena battle in which he defended his title against Artie Levine, described as a "walk-in, hands-down hooker from Brooklyn." Robinson was knocked down in an early round, but was saved by the bell. He came back and kayoed Levine.

Eddie Coen described the see-saw battle as "the greatest fight I ever saw" in Bob Dolgan's recollections of highlights of the Arena's history.

Coen remembered that Al Sutphin liked to open up the building to ice skating clubs, and that Walt Trimmer would play the organ as couples would glide on the ice after hockey games or on Sunday mornings. "Sometimes there would be so many people on the ice you couldn't see it."

Coen reminisced about the time the Barons won a Calder Cup by accident. It seems Bobby Crystal, a Barons defenseman, was so exhausted during an overtime game with Pittsburgh that he tried to flip the puck down the ice so he could go to the bench and get a rest, according to Coen. "But the puck bounced past Goalie Gil Mayer for the winning goal!"

With the rays from its golden past still settled on the Arena, the dark news of the trouble within dismayed the Champ, still an active player on the Cleveland and Florida scene.

His own relationship with the Arena purchasers had begun to sour not long after the deal had been completed. He had not wanted to make the hockey team part of the deal, for one thing. They had been his personal property long before there was an Arena, but the prospective buyers balked at the idea of acquiring the building without the team. Sutphin conceded the issue of his team ownership as to spoil the larger deal. In similar way, he included ownership of the Braden-Sutphin building. People who were close to him detected certain signs of regret over those terms later, especially when the new owners began to hike the numbers in the proposed renewal of the lease in the mid-1950's.

The Champ touched on the situation in a personal letter to his son, Jimmy, in 1960:

"Have your notation in which you mention that Bill Lavery is on his way out as Manager of the Cleveland Arena. This was inevitable. Understand that the boys in Detroit who own the Arena...were really burned up at Bill's handling of the Braden-Sutphin renewal lease...Lavery insisted that I would never move, and that I would stand still for a $65,000 a year rental. He insisted that a move elsewhere would cost us about a quarter-of-a-million dollars, and that I was not the kind of a guy who would spend that at my age...

Little did they know of your father, who can be kissed into anything, but can be forced into nothing. Needless to mention, that our old quarters in the Chester Building have been unoccupied and unwanted for two-and-a-half years."

Sutphin's refusal to agree to the terms of the proposed new lease was no bluff. He moved Braden-Sutphin Ink Company out of the Chester

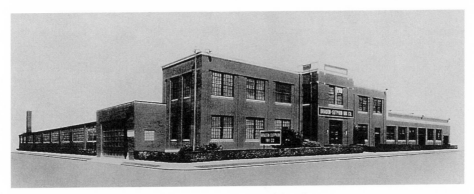

The new Braden-Sutphin plant

Avenue facility to a building on E. 93rd Street. It was an expensive move, but he was determined not to yield to the Arena owners. They had played a game of chicken with the Champ and they had lost. The building vacated by the ink company was torn down shortly thereafter.

The transfer of the ink plant was more than just a physical shift. The Chester Avenue site was Al Sutphin's last tangible link with the Arena past and its abandonment was a sentimental rupture for him personally. The building was a constant reminder of all the nostalgic recollections of the heyday of the Sutphin enterprises.

Mingled with those pleasant memories, however, was the recollection of the bitter months when the employees of the ink company went on strike. That happened in the winter of 1958-59. The labor stoppage was brought about by an attempt to organize the Braden-Sutphin employees, some 80 in number. The Teamsters Union maintained a picket line around the plant during the two months' duration of the walkout and some violence erupted before the strike ended. The company management was able to claim a victory, but the Champ was personally disheartened by the unpleasant episode that had pitted friend against friend. After all, Sutphin was on intimate terms with almost all the people on the payroll.

The ink company's departure from its Chester Avenue building exacerbated the already serious crisis being faced by the owners of the Arena. From 1962 until 1974, Lemmo, as General Manager, struggled valiantly to keep the ship afloat, staying at his post to the bitter end.

In 1974, the Arena closed its doors by order of its new owner, Cleveland sports promoter Nick Mileti, who had risen, in meteoric style, from

assistant prosecutor in Lakewood to the Cleveland sports mogul. He not only bought the Arena and the Barons, he had taken over the Cleveland Indians baseball team from Vernon Stouffer, purchased the most powerful radio station in the city and had secured a Cleveland franchise in the N.B.A.

Mileti did not acquire ownership of the Arena and the Barons with any intention of restoring them to their former grandeur. His eyes were on a distant horizon and

Nick Mileti & his Richfield Colesium

a more ambitious plan. What he had in mind was construction of a new sports "Coliseum" in the little township of Richfield, some 25 miles south of Cleveland, reaping fans and profits from the entire Cleveland-Akron area.

With the completion of the Coliseum in Richfield in 1974, the Cleveland Arena no longer had a reasonable chance of survival. Mileti's Barons and Cavaliers were transferred to Richfield. The lights on the Arena marquee went out and the great building, still one of the finest facilities of its kind, closed its doors.

There followed three years of rumor and controversy as the fate of the Arena hung in the balance. There was general agreement that it was much too valuable a facility to abandon, much too young a structure to die, but there was also was a general show of timidity. Nobody wanted to be saddled with the financial burden.

Mileti shopped the building around at a reported asking price of $1,400,000. It could not have been duplicated for 20 times that amount, but there were no takers.

The Cleveland city administration under Mayor Ralph Perk recognized that the Arena was an important civic asset with enormous potential as a center for scholastic and collegiate sports and public gatherings. The political leadership and the business establishment were also aware that the permanent loss of the Arena would be a terrible blow to upper Euclid Avenue, already in a state of decline. But the city's bid to buy the

Arena was successfully opposed by some social activists who argued that the million dollars in available federal money would be better spent on community neighborhoods. Suggestions that the Arena would be an ideal acquisition for the fledgling Cleveland State University, whose campus was hardly more than a block away, aroused little official support.

Razing the Arena (1974)

All of the ideas and proposals came to naught. The great edifice, still in its physical prime, stood empty for about three years while would-be buyers ruefully circled the deal and finally shrugged it off as a poor risk. There was the ever-present reality that the thousands of Clevelanders who once would filled the Arena's stands had gone south. To Richfield.

All that the Arena had left to command respect was its imposing physical presence and its storied past. But forty years of memories would bring nothing on the commercial market.

So it was that in April, 1977, wrecking crews began to tear down the House that Al Built. They did a thorough job. When they were finished, the site was nothing more than a vacant lot that Mileti donated to his alma mater, Bowling Green State University. That far-off institution, having no use for an empty field on a fast decaying avenue, sold the property for $330,000 to the American Red Cross. The modest area headquarters of the Red Cross remain on the site today.

Experts say that a building such as the Arena could not be duplicated today for less than $50 million. Its sorry fate, in retrospect, is quite unbelievable. The wrecker's ball did more than destroy a great facility. Much of Euclid Avenue crumbled under those heavy blows.

Gund Arena

It appears now that Al Sutphin was right when he said that Cleveland needed his Arena and that Nick Mileti was wrong when he said the city would be better served by a facility some 25 miles to the south. The twenty years that have elapsed between the end of the Arena era and the finale of the Coliseum's active role have resolved the issue.

A new arena has risen in the city's downtown Gateway complex, another at the south end of the CSU campus, both costly undertakings for the city and the taxpayers. The comment has been made many times and echoed from city hall to corporate boardrooms to countless corner bars—"It's a shame they tore down the Arena."

Al Sutphin would be hard pressed to disagree.

C.S.U. Convocation Center

THE GLORY YEARS

Season	W	L	Results
1937-38	25	12	Won division Lost in 1st round of playoff
1938-39	23	22	3rd place in division **Won 1st Calder Cup**
1939-40	24	24	4th place in division Missed playoff
1940-41	26	21	Won division **Won 2nd Calder Cup**
1941-42	33	19	3rd place in division Lost in 2nd round of playoff
1942-43	21	29	6th place in division Lost in 2nd round of playoff
1943-44	33	14	Won division Lost in final round of playoff
1944-45	34	16	Won division **Won 3rd Calder Cup**
1945-46	28	26	3rd place in division Lost in final round of playoff
1946-47	38	18	Won division Lost in 1st round of playoff
1947-48	43	13	Won division **Won 4th Calder Cup**
1948-49	41	21	3rd place in division Lost in 2nd round of playoff

| Total
12 years | 369 | 235 | .611 winning percentage
6 Division championships
4 League championships |

Overleaf: Mary Hoynes Sutphin, circa 1950

CHAPTER NINETEEN

BEHIND IT ALL, MARY STOOD TALL

There was little doubt in the minds of Al Sutphin's boyhood friends that some day he would make something special of himself. After all, for as long as they could remember, he was the leader, the promoter, the dreamer, the charmer. But what of his bride of more than fifty years, Mary Althea Hoynes? Could anyone have surmised that this rather quiet and unassuming daughter of Mike and Florence Hoynes would play such a significant role in her husband's many achievements?

From the outset of their marriage Mary was totally involved in the entertainment side of selling ink. Her natural sense for organization and marvelous Irish wit were the perfect complement for Al, the human dynamo. Together they copyrighted that amazing and very personal "Sutphin touch" which captivated friends and customers alike.

In fact, during their initial twelve months of wedded bliss, Mary planned and executed thirty formal dinner parties at the Hoynes' home, serving over 350 guests.

By the early 1930's the Sutphins were getting their initial experience at welcoming business friends for weekend visits to their summer home at East 185th and Lakeshore Blvd. Planning meals, sleeping arrangements and entertainment for their numerous guests became part of Mary's weekly agenda. In 1933 the family moved to their spacious home on Berkshire Road in Cleveland Heights and the art of entertaining "Sutphin style" moved into high gear.

During the early days of the Arena, the Sutphin home was open every Saturday night after hockey games to as many as one hundred visitors. Mary employed a wonderful Swedish caterer, Marie, to assist her in the preparations for customary 11:30 p.m. arrivals. Festivities often lasted past 2:00 a.m. with overnight visitors more the rule than the exception. That usually led to Sunday brunches followed by a frenzied effort to put the house back in order.

Braden-Sutphin business associates, friends, Arena investors, newspaper writers, radio broadcasters and sports celebrities visited the Berk-

...from the Sutphin Family Christmas Album, December 7, 1941

shire residence regularly. It was commonplace for Mary to receive a phone call from the Champ requesting last-minute arrangements be made for backyard clambakes, cookouts and overnight guests. Once, during the 1947-48 hockey season, seven young Canadian players were bivouacked on the third floor for ten days while more permanent living quarters could be secured. These young men were away from their small Canadian towns and villages for the first time. In her own gracious and unassuming way, Mary made these 17 and 18 year olds feel completely at home. But then, that was standard fair for Mary Sutphin.

Beginning in the summer of 1941 and continuing until 1953, the two five-bedroom cottages in Kingstown, Ontario became a favorite spot of the Sutphins. They usually arrived by mid-June, staying until school opened in fall.

Once again, the organizational skills of Mary Sutphin were put to the test. As at the Florida Farm, the usual mix of guests were invited to Kingston for ten-day periods. Each morning, Mary shopped Kingston's open air markets and butchery. She developed a wonderful rapport with all the local shopkeepers, farmers and trades people. No doubt, Mary was a major cog in Kingston's summer economy and everyone felt her absence when she departed for Cleveland each September.

Kingston was also the scene for one of the family's boldest pranks. It would turn out to be one of Mary's greatest embarrassments.

Bill Tobin, owner of the Chicago Blackhawks hockey club, and his wife Barney were annual guests at Kingston. They dearly loved the Sutphin brood, and Bill took great delight in teasing the six children, especially young Jimmy.

On this particular occasion, Tobin arrived and immediately requested that Jimmy assist him with one of his bags. The young man, a fine wrestler at University School in Cleveland, strained and struggled as he dragged the suitcase up the steep hill, through the cot-

The Berkshire Road House

tage and up the stairs. Tobin followed close behind, and, upon reaching his room, unceremoniously reprimanded the boy. "You grabbed the wrong bag," he scolded. The bewildered Jimmy took up the load and quickly returned it to the front of the house. Whereupon, in full view of family, guests and the exhausted teenager, Tobin unpacked the bag, revealing a dozen large paving stones. Everyone howled ... and no one more than Bill Tobin. Not surprisingly, Jimmy was not so amused.

The patient Sutphins waited for their chance to retaliate. Tobin soon provided them the opportunity. It so happened that in addition to being an avid fisherman, Bill loved the game of golf. When he had finished his ten day stint at Kingston, Tobin took a train to Montreal for several days of hockey meetings and discovered he had left his golf clubs in the Champ's car. Bill called Al and requested that Jimmy bring the clubs and meet his train when it passed through Kingston on its way to Toronto. Sutphin assured him that they'd take care of him...and then went to work.

The Champ instructed Alberta and Jimmy to fish the lake for a dozen rock bass. The day's catch was carefully placed in the bottom of Tobin's golf bag. Sutphin replaced the clubs, zipped the bag's travel cover and sent Jimmy to the station to meet Tobin. The unsuspecting Bill was generous in his thanks for all the young man's efforts. When Tobin arrived home in Chicago, he returned the golf bag to its customary spot on his back porch. With the hockey season upon him, Bill knew it would be spring before he played again.

The Tobins & the Sutphins in Kingston, Ont.

Approximately six weeks later, Mary Sutphin (now back in Cleveland), received a call from her good friend Barney Tobin. She had long since forgotten the "going away" present that Champ and Jimmy had bestowed on Bill. Barney proceeded to describe in graphic detail what had transpired.

In the last few weeks an unctuous smell had permeated the entire first floor of their home. Exterminators pinpointed the back porch and believed an animal had burrowed under it and died. Bill had torn apart more than half the porch before he moved his golf bag. Only then did he determine the source of the rank odor and realize he'd been victimized by Al and company.

For a moment Mary was too stunned to offer even a meek apology. She feared the prank might jeopardize her wonderful friendship with the Tobins. Fortunately, Barney's great sense of humor held true to form. She reassured Mary that all was well. As for Bill, the incident permanently cured him of his penchant for teasing the Sutphin children. That Christmas, Mary made sure that Albert presented Bill Tobin with new golf clubs and a bag.

The indelible mark Mary left on the thousands of guests at Fort Myers from 1938 until 1985 has already been chronicled here. What has not, however, was the interesting relationship Mary had with Ruth Galvin, Al's carefully chosen kitchen manager in the early 1950's.

When Mary's daughter, Mary Elizabeth, was asked how her mother received the news of Galvin's hiring, she broke out in laughter.

"Boy, it really hit the fan! Mother was furious with Dad. It would be like telling your wife you had put your children up for adoption! Running the farm was Mother's domain and the introduction of Ruth Galvin was a major invasion of her turf.   Prior to that, Mother would attend the 6:30 Mass in town, pick up the kitchen helpers and drive nine miles back to the Farm. Then it was back to Fort Myers to visit all her merchant friends to procure that day's provisions. When she returned to the property in the afternoon, she assisted with the cooking, planned the next day's meals and activities and greeted the many guests. Dad just felt it was time to give Mother some assistance before she completely wore out. With Ruth Galvin on the scene, the town's merchants were suddenly delivering to the Farm—Ruth knew all of them from her days at the Fort Myers Country Club. It had never occurred to Mother to ask them to do so. Though it took a long time, Mother and Ruth eventually passed the point of peaceful co-existence to reach a deep mutual respect for one another.

It was no surprise that Mrs. Galvin and Mary eventually got along, for Mary was that rare person who found a way to get along with everyone. People gravitated to this thoughtful, quiet woman, confided in her and sought her advice on matters great and small. On more than one occasion while living on Berkshire, she carried dinner to homes of neighbors with newborns or some family crisis. She was a favorite of her children's friends because of her warmth and good humor. She showed great respect for others, especially those who worked in the Sutphin household. As Mary Elizabeth told it, "We never had a cook or maid who wasn't crazy about her. Her attitude was, 'we can always have more children, but it's not easy to find good help.'"

Mary's quiet charm concealed a remarkable bold streak. Who else would have had the audacity to take on both Paul Brown and the Champ? One Poem Night at the Farm, Mary went into the kitchen of the Casino where Norbert Stein, Bill Summers and others were arguing over who would have the nerve to conclude their skit by racing through the kitchen's swinging door to throw a Boston cream pie at dear Coach Paul. Mary never hesitated. She grabbed the pie, flew through the door, took aim and scored. Brown joked about the incident for years, still amazed that such an elegant lady could perform so dastardly a deed.

And imagine the expression on Al's face the night he was victimized. One evening the Champ was pontificating on a topic Mary preferred not to discuss at the dinner table—report cards. While Mary was serving a dessert of ginger bread covered with whipped cream from a spray can, Al's discourse reached high gear. Suddenly, Sutphin was splattered with whipped cream as Mary stumbled serving his plate. Al forever questioned the accidental nature of his wife's misstep.

Mary also showed her true grit when she decided to learn to drive. The Champ wasn't wild about women driving and had never made an effort to teach her. When Al dismissed a salesman just before his departure for a European vacation, Mary seized the opportunity. She sent Gramma Hoynes' chauffeur to the Braden-Sutphin plant to commandeer the former salesman's car and accompany her to the quiet, outer reaches of Shaker Heights, where she was given her first and only driving lesson. Encouraged by her children, Mary ventured onto the streets of Cleveland during the next several days. A quick learner, Mary was fast becoming an accomplished driver until a minor mishap on Cedar Hill—too fast a startup caused a rear end collision with another car. The other driver calmly got out of his car, picked up Mary's bumper from the street and passed it through her back window to the delight of her three howling daughters.

Despite that setback, Mary persevered. When Albert returned from Europe a month later she met him at the train station. The Champ could only stare in shock and disbelief when he saw his bride at the wheel of his beloved Cadillac convertible!

Much has been made of the delight Al Sutphin took in playing practical jokes, with Mary and Norbert Stein as his leading co-conspirators. Some of the best were initiated by these two, working independently from the master.

Mary credited Norbert for the their all-time escapade, executed with her blessing and co-operation, which was pulled on Paul Brown during the *Queen Elizabeth's* Atlantic crossing in the spring of 1959.

The Browns had suffered crushing back-to-back losses to New York, ending the 1958 season. Andy Robustelli, the Giants all-pro defensive end, had two career games, contributing mightily to the Browns demise. The Champ and Brown were traveling to Europe with their wives, at least partially in an effort to take Paul's mind off the ignominious defeats. Imagine Brown's reaction when every waiter, bus boy, deck hand, and crewman donned a replica of Robustelli's #81 jersey (courtesy of Norbert) as soon as the ship had left port!

It should come as no surprise that Mary and Norbert, in a generous spirit of fair play, would occasionally turn on each other, especially on that hallowed feast of jesters, April Fools Day.

It was the early 1940's, during the Champ's hockey heyday, and Sutphin was headed to the West Coast. He impulsively decided that, rather than travel by train directly back to Cleveland, he would take a more circuitous return route so he could check up on the efforts of his hockey scouts. Sutphin wanted to go north into Canada and then east through dozens of small towns, returning through Minnesota. For Stein, Al's traveling secretary, this meant the nightmarish task of adding all the extra stops and procuring train tickets. The ticket package itself stretched over ten feet. The exhausted Norbert had just returned home from spending his entire day rescheduling the Champ's journey when his telephone rang. It was Mary Sutphin.

STEIN REAL BRAINS BEHIND AL'S EMPIRE

Norbert's practical jokes never stopped...

"Norbert", she asked, "have you started working on Albert's itinerary yet?"

"Started?" he growled. "I've spent twelve hours sorting out this mess!"

"Oh, what a shame. I've just received a telegram from Albert. He's decided to reverse his trip, starting in Minnesota then going west through Canada."

There was a prolonged silence as Stein listened. Finally, he exploded. "That's it! I've had it with that guy! Wire him and tell him, 'I quit!'"

"Oh, that won't be necessary, Norbert", Mary gleefully explained. "April Fools!".

It took Stein several years to get his revenge but it was worth the wait. Mary's youngest son, Cal, was going to Fort Myers High School and had invited a local girl to the Senior Dance. Though it was nothing serious, Mary was concerned. She knew many of the girls in Fort Myers married right out of high school. The Sutphins had great hopes for Cal and marrying young was definitely not part of the plan. Aware of all this, Norbert launched his scheme when he visited the Farm that weekend, just as Mary had departed for Cleveland. A day later, Stein sent her a telegram announcing that Cal and his date had eloped and would contact Mary when they returned from their honeymoon! The telegram was signed, "Love, Cal." Poor Mary was near hysterics. Stein did not help matters any when he failed to call to expose the joke. After that, Mary refrained from any further one-upsmanship with nasty old Norbert on the first of April.

Certainly to the outside world it was the charm, wit and uncanny ability to bring order to chaos that set Mary Sutphin apart. For her family, it was much more than that. She had an unwavering inner strength fueled by an Irish Catholic faith, the solid foundation underlying all her accomplishments. Her day always began with early morning Mass and Communion, and usually ended with the Rosary.

Her son, Jim, remembered that "Mother thought that going through life was like riding a tandem bicycle, God in the front steering the way. She remained in back doing the pedaling."

Mary Althea Hoynes Sutphin managed to get in a lot of pedaling.

While raising six children, she found time to visit and care for her sister, Florence, who suffered with tuberculosis and spent much of her life at Sunny Acres Sanatorium. When Mary contracted the disease herself, she insisted on recovering at home where she could at least oversee the well-being of her family.

Her bubbly enthusiasm for living and determined faith somehow kept her going. Daughter Mary E. recalled that "Mother's faith certainly rubbed off on all of us. And it was never tedious or boring because it was so practical in its application to everyday life. She believed that if you wanted something you prayed about it and went about doing all the right things to accomplish that goal. If it was part of God's plan for you, then it would come to fruition. Yet, if it did not happen, it was only because God had a better plan, another door to open to you, and you would probably never know what you had missed. God would provide for you in another way."

Mary Sutphin's spirituality had an impact on all her grandchildren and great grandchildren. In the early 1970's one of her grandsons was diagnosed with bone cancer. In the weeks and months that followed he was overwhelmed with cards, letters and prayers of encouragement from her and all her friends at the Farm. She also called on every priest, nun and religious order she knew to enlist their prayer support. Mary was hardly surprised when he was restored to health after a lengthy battle with the disease.

Another of her grandchildren, Mary Dana Leitch, also has fond memories of her grandmother's rich faith life. As a child, she often accompanied Mary Sutphin to St. Anne's Church in Cleveland Heights for 6:30 Mass. On more than one occasion, Mary Dana was told by her grandmother "how lucky she was to have been born Catholic 'now-a-days' ... it used to be they'd feed them to the lions."

Mary had 28 grandchildren in all

In 1977 Mary Dana moved to the Farm with her daughter, Heather, and spent many rewarding hours with Grandma. As Mary Dana recalled it, "It was the lowest point in my life, a time when nothing made sense to me and I was desperately searching for answers. Grandma's still abiding faith, her firmness and Irish sense of humor—all the things I enjoyed so much as a child —brought me back from the ragged edge of my own destruction. Her faith in me led me to believe in myself again.".

Daughter, sister, wife, mother, grandmother, great grandmother, friend, gracious hostess. Mary Sutphin assumed all these roles in her eighty-nine years of abundant living.

As those who knew her best and loved her most gathered to say farewell in November of 1985, the matriarch of the Sutphin family was eulogized in the memorable words of her son, Jim:

"We have lost our spiritual leader. Mary Althea Hoynes Sutphin was a rock...and it was on that very solid foundation that this family was built." The Champ himself couldn't have said it better.

Overleaf: "Champ" at 75!

CHAPTER TWENTY

A CHAMP TO THE END

The Sutphin Family's 1960 Christmas card was different from any of those that had preceded it in this long-standing holiday tradition. Instead of the usual season's wishes, it was an open letter from the Champ to his "many fine friends."

Al had suffered a heart attack in December, a serious and distressing development that was more than offset by the incredible outpouring of love and sympathy from friends and colleagues.

"Normally," he wrote in his Christmas message, "I take a dim view of form letters, but in this case I truly rejoice that our friends made this form letter a necessity. While in the hospital...I received over twelve hundred letters and cards...and dozens and dozens of phone calls were made to my Mary.

"And it is a physical impossibility for me to convey personally and individually my sincere thanks for your friendly graciousness...."

He went on to thank specific people and groups who had meant so much to him in his lifetime, starting with individuals with whom he had been associated some 30 years before.

"I was pleased by the messages received from my old employees and associates at the Cleveland Arena...it was nice to be remembered by them twelve years later.

"Please know it was gratifying indeed receiving such wonderful messages of concern from the 102 employees and associates of mine at Braden-Sutphin.

"And will always be grateful to my old friends in radio and television who announced my predicament, Sunday after Sunday, from coast-to-coast....Oh, this was very kind.

"I will be eternally grateful to the Cleveland newspapers who ran practically a Box Score of my progress..."

He went on to thank his old army buddies of the 135th Artillery, the many customers of Braden-Sutphin, and "those 500 little Sandlot Ball Players who individually signed a glorious plaque urging my speedy recovery."

The Champ (1961)

He concluded by advising everybody that "Anyone having so many fine friends has much to live for."

The Champ bounced back, just as everyone who knew him was sure he would. Perhaps he was more determined than ever to extract the last full measure from life.

His battle to stave off the new bridge to Cape Coral brought out his old fighting spirit, and there were politicians in Fort Myers who wished they had never heard of the bridge by the time Sutphin had vented his fury on them. Two county commissioners were ousted at the polls in what was widely considered punishment for their part in sponsoring the bridge.

There were more European trips, and, above all, there was the Farm. The hordes of guests and endless cycle of entertainment and surprises continued unabated.

In his later years, the Champ finally found the time to repay the debt of time he owed his family. His enduring regret over too many long days in the office and extended intervals away from home was turned to joy when, at last, he lavished attention on the ones he loved, which now included not only his six children but over two dozen fortunate members of the next generation of Sutphins.

For most kids growing up, there is no more wonderful person imaginable than Santa Claus. But if you were one of Al Sutphin's 28 grandchildren or his "adopted" grandchildren (like the Fords and

McManamons), Santa Claus was a make-believe character who paled in comparison to this gregarious man in the bright red tie. They were his special little people and nothing was more important to him.

The Alcazar Hotel was the scene for an endless cavalcade of Halloween, Christmas, and birthday parties. Each Christmas, the Champ took over the entire F.A.O. Schwartz toy store for a day so the kids could shop for themselves. He led excursions to Indians games, Euclid Beach and the Cleveland Zoo. During the summer he was the number one fan at Little League games.

The lucky little ones learned gin rummy and shuffleboard in their own private "Garden of Eden"—the Farm at Fort

The Champ & his pals at F.A.O. Schwartz on Shaker Square

Myers. And he plastered their funny faces on his annual Christmas card so he could brag about them to his thousands of friends and customers.

Who could compete with a grandfather like that? When the Champ pulled up in the bright red Cadillac convertible, every boy and girl on the block came visiting—usually wearing something shocking red—in the hope that Mr. Sutphin would bestow on them a brand new $1 bill.

In spite of all this extravagance, Al Sutphin is more fondly remembered for something much more valuable that he and Mary gave their grandchildren. By word, deed and example, they testified to a belief in life's simple truths. Dream your dreams and work tirelessly to achieve them; treat others even better than you would want them to treat you; share all you have with others because it will come back to you in abundance; be grateful for what you've been given; and finally, cultivate a sense of humor so you never take yourself too seriously or fail to laugh at life's good fortune and occasional heartaches.

This was their heritage, and their greatest gift of all.

As the years passed, there was an inevitable readjustment in the lives of Al and Mary. College, marriage, business, and all the other rival attractions that arrive with adulthood tugged at the perimeter of the family circle. The grand house on Berkshire was suddenly too big. Al and Mary moved into an apartment in the Alcazar Hotel. It became their home base as they continued to divide their time between Cleveland and Florida, with extended trips to Europe thrown in for good measure.

A few years later, in 1966, Mary suffered a serious accident. She fell and broke her hip while shopping in a neighborhood supermarket.

In a typical show of independence, she waved aside the helping hands of clerks and customers and managed to get back on her feet. Somehow, she made her way to the checkout counter and said to the manager, "I think I have hurt myself. Would you be so kind as to help me to my car?"

By the time she arrived at the Alcazar, she had begun to realize the extent of her injury. The pain was so excruciating that she didn't even try to get out of her car, simply instructing the doorman to summon Al. He came down, coattails flying, and rushed her to Huron Road Hospital where it was quickly determined that her hip was badly fractured.

Dr. Ivan Lust, longtime team physician for the Barons, operated on Mary. The hip surgery was successful but a life-threatening kidney infection set in. Mary's condition was grave. At the lowest hours in that crisis, the family kept a vigil in the hospital hall, tensely awaiting word.

"I think Mom is going to make it," blurted young Jim. "She's tough!"

Dr. Lust nodded his agreement. "Anyone who could live with your father for 40 years has got to be tough!"

They were both right. Mary recovered completely, and, after a remarkably brief period of convalescence, took command of the Sutphin household once again. It seemed to those around her that she was stronger than ever. Part of that impression may have been due to the perceptible decline in the Champ's condition in the last few years of the decade.

There was no denying that the inescapable slowdown had taken place, but it was made more noticeable because of the contrast with his vibrant past. It was like an Olympic figure skater putting on the brakes in the middle of a triple axel.

At the time, everybody in the family was looking to the big year ahead: 1972, the year that would mark 50 years of marriage for Al and Mary; a golden anniversary that would need no polishing.

But if the Family thought that the Champ, now mostly confined to a wheel chair, was going to accept a passive role in the planning of the big occasion, he soon established his familiar role as commander-in-chief.

The momentous date was August 14th, and everyone in the now largely expanded Sutphin family planned to be at the Farm in Fort Myers for the celebration. Al, typically, decided how they would get there. He

The Sutphin Express, August 1972

didn't trust his loved ones to flying machines. The loss of Jim Braden in an air crash long ago still affected him. The plea went out to one and all: no flying, please.

What he proposed was that everybody ride to Fort Myers from Cleveland in a chartered bus. There was no resistance as the idea actually sounded like fun: 40 family members would start the party early, riding nonstop, straight through from Cleveland to Fort Myers, pausing only for rest stops, food and fuel.

"What an incredible trip!" said Jim Sutphin. "Anybody who made that junket will never forget it, and they will probably never forget Harry Leitch and Norbert Stein playing cards all the way, through two nights!"

The only thing lacking was the Champ himself aboard, crying out "Panorama! Panorama!" when some spectacular view came within sight.

Altogether, some 101 guests were on hand at the Farm to help Mary and Al celebrate.

August 14, 1972 turned out to be an unforgettable night. The

Farm never looked more attractive. A five-foot high fountain, brilliantly lighted, splashed away in a central setting, surrounded by outdoor tables and chairs for the guests. The scene was a replica of the Champ's favorite restaurant in Paris, with strolling violinists adding to the ambiance.

The most spectacular part of the celebration was Mary Sutphin's gift to her husband that night—a 30-minute display of fireworks that lit

Al & Mary in the golden years

up the Farm and the Caloosahatchie River and startled all the drivers passing by on the villainous Cape Coral bridge. Even the Champ, a man used to springing the big surprises, was thrilled.

All of the family members came away with vivid memories of the last of the great parties in Fort Myers. Jim Sutphin's most cherished recollection is this: "We were all crowded into the Casino for this very, very nice dinner that was arranged by my sisters. My dad was not in good health. He could hardly get around. His hips were really bothering him. His eyes were bad. He had diabetes. He just wasn't in good shape.

"My mother was just full of pep. She had all kinds of energy. No problems. She was constantly taking care of my father, like cleaning his glasses; all kinds of stuff."

On the formal program, Mary Sutphin yielded to the entreaties of her children and gave a brief, witty talk, heartfelt and heartwarming.

"Then Dad got up. Mind you, he could hardly get out of his wheelchair. Leaning on his cane, he looked around and said: 'Well, it's obvious, isn't it? I was better to her than she was to me!'

"It brought the house down. He was always good at saying the right thing at the right time."

The Sutphin's 50th Anniversary
standing, l. to r., Sandy Sutphin, Alberts Stoney, Carolyn Leitch, Jane
Leitch, Ray Stoney, Bob Leitch, Harry Leitch, seated, l. to r., Louise
Sutphin, Mary, Al, Jim Sutphin & Cal Sutphin

Limited as he had to be, the Champ nevertheless took an active role, and his contribution, as might have been expected, centered on baseball. With Norbert Stein's help, he set up a schedule of games spread out over two of the three days of the anniversary celebration. His love of organization would not permit just casual games played on some street corner lot. He made arrangements for the contests to be played at Terry Park, the spring training field of the Pittsburgh Pirates. An American Legion team of all-stars was recruited to provide some competition for the Sutphin grandchildren. The Champ also ordered special uniforms for all the players.

Terry Park was a Sutphin playground on those two days of golden anniversary baseball. The two day "Sutphin Series" at Terry Park was a showcase for the third generation of Sutphins to show their granddad how well they could play, and what they had learned about winning.

The Sutphin All-Stars
standing, l. to r., Hal Leitch, Rob Leitch, Tim Leitch, Ray Stoney, Jr.,
Jeff Leitch, Matt Stoney, kneeling, l. to r., Bill Leitch, Dan Leitch, Al,
Jamie Sutphin, Jim Leitch

Some of the younger Sutphin children gave added authenticity to the occasion by selling popcorn in the stands. The Champ himself sat in his wheel chair on the sideline and plainly enjoyed the spectacle taking place all around him. A stray ball hit him in the chest once, but he hardly seemed to notice it. He was in his element.

The Sutphin "Senior" All-Stars
standing, l. to r., Larry Ford, Ray Stoney, Sr., Norbert Stein, Bob Leitch,
Harry Leitch, Tom McManamon, kneeling, l. to r., David
McManamon, Patrick MaManamon, Al, Jim Sutphin, Cal Sutphin

On the second day of the celebration, the same grandchildren took on a team of old friends and family members. The "senior" lineup included Norbert Stein, Harry and Bob Leitch, Ray Stoney, Jim and Cal Sutphin, and Tom McManamon. This one was a softball game, a concession to creaking limbs and stiff joints. Even for Florida, the August heat was extraordinary, and the older players wisely consumed large amounts of Gatorade, a drink favored by athletes, especially when spiked with gin.

The adult's good cheer seemed undiminished by the loss of that historic game. Upon their return to the Farm, they celebrated their defeat by jumping into the pool, still wearing their uniforms!

That 50th anniversary celebration was more than the formal recognition of the long and successful union of Mary Hoynes and Al Sutphin. It was also a showcase for the most enduring result of that marriage, the children and grandchildren. Much of what the Champ had a hand in creating—such as the Arena—no longer existed, as if in testimony to the transitory nature of man's works. All around him, in living contrast, was the large family that he and Mary had brought into being. There could have been no more fitting tribute than this reunion on the Farm. It was a climactic event. Afterward, Al took on a serene sense of resignation, an acknowledgment that this was a time of quiet epilogue at the end of an incredibly productive and generous life.

The Champ died at the age of 80 on June 25, 1974. Like all who knew him well, Jim Sutphin has the day fixed in memory.

"It was almost like the heavens cried. It really, really rained in Cleveland. The day was dark and miserable...It was as if somebody special had left this earth."

The tributes and condolences poured in from all sides.

"The name of Sutphin," said the *Cleveland Plain Dealer*, "always will have a deserved high place in Cleveland's sports history."

Looking back over an extraordinarily full and rewarding life, the Champ himself might well have nodded in agreement, puffed on his pipe, straightened his red tie and summed it all up in one of his many memorable sayings.

"Panorama, everyone!"

Overleaf: "Champ"

EPILOGUE

It was a particularly warm late Florida afternoon and Al Sutphin was seated by his pool overlooking the Caloosahatchee River. He was engaged in an animated dialogue with good friend and successful Cleveland businessman, Frank Blasko. They were discussing their respective businesses and the various nuances peculiar to each enterprise. Frank, probably thirty years the Champ's junior, was particularly curious about their comparative operating expenses, labor rates, and Sutphin's obvious long-term success marketing printing ink. The conversation had reached its climax and Blasko was hoping to glean some pearl that could prove especially fruitful to his own career. "Al, he asked, "just what is ink made of ?" Sutphin turned toward Blasko, his eyes narrowing and took a long drag on his El Verso cigar. Then turning back toward the setting sun he blew out several rings of blue smoke. "What's ink made of?" With just the slightest trace of a smile the Champ answered him. "Water and profit, Frank, ...but mostly profit."

George Condon

Jeffrey T. Leitch

ABOUT THE AUTHOR

It was a Friday in April of 1991 and the Cleveland Indians were holding their annual Kickoff Luncheon to welcome the start of another baseball season. At a nearby table sat Hal Lebovitz, columnist for the *Lake County News Herald*, and for many years the sports Editor of Cleveland's *Plain Dealer*. I had met Hal in the summer of 1973 while working part-time in the Indian's press box. At that time I had boldly introduced myself as Al Sutphin's grandson; Lebovitz was gracious and asked how Al and Mary Sutphin were doing. He laughingly explained how he had refereed the first professional basketball game at the Arena in 1946 and how it became a complete fiasco. Players were slipping and sliding every which way as moisture accumulated on the basketball floor that had been put down on top of the Arena's ice. One of the few times Al Sutphin was left speechless, Hal said. Though I knew he would not remember me, nearly twenty years later I was approaching Lebovitz at the end of the luncheon to ask his advise about a project I was considering: namely, to have a book written about my grandfather. Hal was kind but very realistic. "Al was a terrific guy whose story is well-worth telling ... but you're really about twenty-five years late" — "finding sources ... identifying your audience" ... "it'll be a tough job." But if we decided to do it, who could he recommend as a potential author? After a long pause Hal asked, "Well, do you know George Condon"? Yes, I knew George. Coincidentally he and his wife Marje lived behind us on the next street in Lakewood. We had been acquaintances since 1985 and had talked about Al Sutphin frequently. Although George did not really know my grandfather he was quite familiar with his accomplishments and was a great admirer of his. For nearly 40 years George had been a feature columnist with the *Plain*

Dealer. He either knew everyone or knew about them - there was no mistake about that. With his Irish wit and charm, George had already spun more than a few good stories for me as we hung "over the fence" sipping a cold drink. And who wasn't familiar with his book, *Cleveland: The Best Kept Secret?* Written in the early 1960's, it was still a most definitive work in understanding our city's great history. My chief concern was that George had better things to do than tackle our project with all its difficulties. During a lunch at Pier W Restaurant in late April, '91 I assessed Condon's interest in the project. Was this really a book worth writing? And could we still do a credible job of telling the unlikely story of a self-made dynamo who rekindled a city's downtown in the midst of the country's worst economic times with a sports Arena and every possible event and promotion? To his credit, George never hesitated. He accepted the challenge and despite the continual "excitement" of working with the Sutphin family, he has produced an informative and entertaining narrative.

So, George, for your boundless energy, patience, creativity, and persistence the Sutphin family, and myself especially, are most grateful for a job well done.

Jeff Leitch